Luan Ferr

Arcturians
Energy Healing

Copyright
Original Title: Arcturians - Energy Healing
Copyright © 2023, published in 2024 by Luiz Antonio dos Santos ME.
This book explores energy healing practices and delves into connections with subtle energies to promote well-being and balance. Its aim is to inspire self-awareness and personal development, offering a comprehensive and practical perspective on the subject. However, it does not replace professional medical or psychological guidance.

Energy Healing
Second Edition

Second Edition Production Team
Author: Luan Ferr
Revision: Virginia Moreira dos Santos
Graphic Design and Layout: Arthur Mendes da Costa
Cover: Anderson Casagrande Neto
Translation: Igor Ramisck

Publication and Identification
Energy Healing / By Luan Ferr
Ahzuria Publishing, 2024
Categories: Body, Mind & Spirit / Spirituality
DDC: 158.1 - CDU: 613.8

Copyright Notice
All rights reserved by:
Booklas Publishing / Luiz Antonio dos Santos ME
This book may not be reproduced, distributed, or transmitted, in whole or in part, by any means, electronic or printed, without the express consent of the copyright holder.

# Summary

Prologue ............................................................. 5
1 Beyond the Known............................................. 8
2 The Mysteries of the Universe .......................... 11
3 Cosmic Messengers............................................ 14
4 The Principles of Consciousness........................ 17
5 The Arcturian Frequency ................................... 20
6 Guardians of Peace............................................. 23
7 Spiritual Evolution ............................................. 26
8 Signs, Symbols, and Channeling........................ 29
9 Cosmic Healing................................................... 32
10 Astral Travel and Dimensional Encounters ..... 35
11 The Ascension of Consciousness..................... 38
12 Unlocking Divine Potential.............................. 41
13 Tools for Transformation ................................. 44
14 Star Children .................................................... 47
15 The Expansion of Consciousness..................... 50
16 Intergalactic Collaboration............................... 53
17 Accessing Higher Dimensions......................... 56
18 Restoring Energetic Balance ............................ 58
19 Planetary Consciousness .................................. 60
20 Ancient Knowledge.......................................... 62
21 Vibrational Transformation.............................. 65
22 Unity in the Multiverse .................................... 67
23 Spiritual Path..................................................... 70
24 Healing and Transforming ............................... 73
25 Attracting Aligned Experiences ....................... 76

26 Collective Consciousness ........................................................ 79
27 Conscious Manifestation ........................................................ 82
28 Journey of the Soul ............................................................... 87
29 Unification of Consciousness ................................................. 91
30 Spiritual Mastery ................................................................... 95
31 Cosmic Purpose ................................................................... 100
32 Expansion of Consciousness ................................................ 103
33 Energetic Harmonization ..................................................... 105
34 Multidimensional Abilities .................................................. 107
35 Galactic Consciousness ........................................................ 115
36 Reconnection with the Source ............................................. 118
37 Arcturian Light .................................................................... 121
38 The Ascension of Humanity ................................................ 123
39 The Cosmic Unity ................................................................ 126
40 Practical Part ....................................................................... 129
41 Channeling .......................................................................... 130
42 Automatic Writing .............................................................. 133
43 Meditation ........................................................................... 135
44 Visualization ....................................................................... 138
45 Speaking in Trance .............................................................. 140
46 Telepathic Communication ................................................. 142
47 Connection with the Inner Self ........................................... 145
48 Connection with .................................................................. 147
49 Stillness ............................................................................... 149
50 Self-Connection .................................................................. 152
51 Energy Healing ................................................................... 154
52 Cosmic Healing ................................................................... 156

53 Astral Travel and Interdimensional Encounters.................... 158
54 Consciousness Expansion .................................................... 161
55 DNA Activation ................................................................... 164
56 Conscious Breathing ........................................................... 166
57 Cellular Regeneration .......................................................... 168
58 Connecting with the Star Child Within................................ 170
59 Accessing the Stellar Portal ................................................. 172
60 Energy Transmutation.......................................................... 174
61 Grounding ............................................................................ 177
62 Arcturian Resonance ............................................................ 179
63 Self-Knowledge ................................................................... 182
64 Recognizing Gifts ................................................................ 185
65 Radiating Arcturian Light .................................................... 187
66 The Ascension of Consciousness......................................... 190
Acknowledgments....................................................................... 193

# Prologue

It doesn't matter your religion, your way of believing, or how you perceive everything around you—your origin is divine, and because it is divine, the energy that permeates everything is always within your reach. We are part of a greater whole.

After extensive research, I discovered that in the most diverse cultures, there is a belief that unseen or unfelt energies control everything around us. Even in cultures entirely different and separated by oceans, their ways of believing in the unseen are essentially identical.

Since time immemorial, cultures around the world have believed in gods who control everything and have performed rituals to gain their favor. This form of faith is ingrained in human DNA; there's no escaping it. We have always believed and will always believe in something superior to ourselves. But humanity has advanced—we no longer live in ignorance.

Scientists might say that what we call religiosity, faith, or whatever name one chooses to use is merely a mental state. Yet, they all agree that when we seek strength in the unknown, our mental state changes, our perception of the world shifts, and miracles happen.

While writing this book about Energy Healing, I became convinced that many ailments do not have their roots in the physical body, even though it is in this physical body that illness manifests. This manifestation occurs because we are beings endowed with five senses, so we only become aware of an illness when it extends beyond the energetic sphere and reaches these senses.

In the pages that follow, we will delve into the depths of energy healing, exploring the mysteries and ancestral practices that permeate different traditions. We will discover how subtle energy can be channeled, directed, and used to promote balance, harmony, and well-being in our lives.

In this book, I will share knowledge about energy healing in a theoretical format, followed by explanations of the techniques related to each practice in the final chapters.

Happy reading!

# 1
# Beyond the Known

There is far more in the vast universe than we can imagine. Within this infinite universe lies a cosmic race known as the Arcturians, extraordinary beings who awaken the curiosity of those seeking to understand the wonders of the cosmos. In this book, we embark on a journey beyond the known, diving into the fascinating world of the Arcturians, from energy healing to the expansion of consciousness.

The Arcturians are an advanced civilization residing in the Arcturus star system, located in the Boötes constellation. Their existence dates back millennia, and they have played a significant role in the spiritual development and evolution of species across the universe. With highly advanced technology and wisdom, the Arcturians are regarded as masters of light and consciousness.

Over time, the Arcturians have been a source of inspiration and guidance for many truth seekers. Their knowledge spans a wide range of topics, from universal laws to energy healing, conscious manifestation, and expanded spirituality. Their wisdom is rooted in understanding the unity of all creation and the power of unconditional love as a transformative force.

A hallmark of the Arcturians is their peaceful and benevolent approach to all forms of life. They recognize the importance of universal harmony and work tirelessly to maintain energetic balance on all levels. The Arcturians are true guardians of peace, dedicated to spreading understanding, compassion, and healing throughout the cosmos.

In addition to their advanced technological capabilities, the Arcturians possess extraordinary psychic and sensory abilities. They are masters of the art of channeling, connecting with other life forms to transmit cosmic messages and guidance. Communication with the Arcturians is often conveyed through symbols, signs, and dreams, opening portals of understanding and revealing profound truths.

By attuning to the Arcturian frequency, one can experience an elevation in consciousness and expand their understanding of the universe. This connection with the Arcturians can lead to spiritual awakening and profound personal transformation. It is as if the boundaries of the known dissolve, allowing the mind and heart to open to a greater and more meaningful reality.

Our journey toward understanding the Arcturians is just beginning. As we delve deeper into their culture, wisdom, and influence, we will immerse ourselves in an ocean of knowledge and experiences that challenge our perceptions and invite us to expand our horizons. Get ready to embark on this incredible adventure and uncover the secrets guarded by the Arcturians as we move closer to a deeper understanding of ourselves and the vast cosmos around us.

# 2
# The Mysteries of the Universe

In the vast and enigmatic universe, each cosmic race has a unique and fascinating story. Let us delve into the mysteries surrounding the origins of the Arcturians, seeking to understand the beginnings and purpose behind their singular existence.

The story of the Arcturians dates back to a time before collective memory. They emerged in an era when the universe was still forming, as stars were being born and planets began to solidify. The Arcturians arose as a race of highly evolved beings whose development is deeply connected to the expansion of consciousness and the pursuit of universal wisdom.

The precise origin of the Arcturians remains a mystery. They believe their roots are intertwined with primordial cosmic forces, manifesting in unique ways throughout their evolution. Some Arcturians believe they are a hybrid species resulting from the crossing of different galactic races, while others hold that they are beings of pure light whose transcendental essence goes beyond physical limitations.

A remarkable characteristic of the Arcturians is their deep connection with spirituality and expanded consciousness. From the early stages of their evolution, they demonstrated a natural affinity for the higher dimensions of knowledge and an intimate understanding of universal laws. Through meditation practices, introspection, and inner search, the Arcturians refined their ability to connect with the divine essence of the universe and access planes of existence beyond human comprehension.

The evolution of the Arcturians was driven by an unceasing quest for truth and the desire to share their wisdom with other cosmic races. Throughout their existence, they have established a network of communication and interaction with civilizations across the galaxy, sharing knowledge, exchanging information, and contributing to mutual growth. The Arcturians have played a fundamental role in shaping and developing many cosmic cultures and societies, leaving their mark in every corner of the universe.

As we explore the origins of the Arcturians, it is important to recognize that their existence transcends time and space. They are multidimensional beings capable of transcending the boundaries of linear time and accessing different realities simultaneously. Their understanding of time is non-linear, allowing them to glimpse the multiple possibilities of the universe and influence the trajectory of cosmic destiny.

Although the Arcturians are an advanced and wise race, they too have faced challenges and obstacles. Over the centuries, they have learned to overcome the limitations of duality and connect with the power of unconditional love as a transformative force. This profound understanding of unity and universal connection is the foundation of their wisdom and guides their path in the universe.

As we delve deeper into the mysteries of the universe and the origins of the Arcturians, we are led to a realm of discoveries and reflections that challenge our conventional understanding. Prepare to expand your horizons and witness the hidden secrets behind the stars as we continue our journey through the cosmic vastness.

# 3
# Cosmic Messengers

The Arcturians have maintained a vibrant connection with Earth, recognizing the importance of our planet as a focal point for transformation and spiritual ascension. The Arcturians see Earth as a school of learning, where souls have the opportunity to experience duality and evolve toward the light.

As cosmic messengers, the Arcturians play a crucial role in communication between different galactic races and humanity. They act as intermediaries, transmitting teachings, guidance, and healing energies. The Arcturians possess a deep understanding of Earth's needs and challenges, and they are committed to assisting in its ascension.

One of the ways the Arcturians connect with humanity is through channeling. They communicate with sensitive and awakened humans, transmitting messages of wisdom, love, and support. Through these channelings, the Arcturians offer valuable guidance for spiritual evolution and the creation of a higher and more harmonious reality.

In addition to direct communication, the Arcturians also send healing energies and frequencies. These energies act as a catalyst for transformation and expansion of consciousness. The Arcturians work closely with elemental beings (the guardians of Earth) to purify and balance the planet's energies, promoting healing and restoring natural harmony.

The Arcturians' presence on Earth is not limited to the energetic realm. They are also known for astral visits and dimensional encounters with those ready to receive them. During these experiences, the Arcturians share advanced teachings, expand consciousness, and activate latent potentials in individuals, accelerating their spiritual growth.

The Arcturians understand the importance of unity and cooperation among different cosmic races. They promote intergalactic collaboration, joining forces with other civilizations to advance spiritual progress and expand consciousness across the universe. The Arcturians remind humanity that we are all interconnected beings, part of a cosmic web of love and light.

As we deepen our understanding of the Arcturians' connection with Earth, we begin to grasp the magnitude of their presence and influence. They are messengers of higher consciousness, reminding us of our divine essence and empowering us to walk the path of spiritual evolution.

Prepare to tune into the energies of the Arcturians, open your heart to their messages, and allow their divine presence to guide you on your journey of awakening. Amid the turbulence and challenges of the world, the Arcturians offer their light and wisdom, reminding us that we are co-creators of a reality founded on love, unity, and expanded consciousness.

# 4
# The Principles of Consciousness

At the core of Arcturian consciousness lies a set of fundamental principles that guide their existence and interaction with the universe. Let us explore these principles and how they manifest in the lives of the Arcturians, highlighting the central role of love and unity in their philosophy.

To the Arcturians, love is the primordial force that permeates the entire cosmos. They understand that love is the divine essence of all that exists and that through love, healing, transformation, and spiritual elevation occur. Love is the fabric that connects all forms of life, transcending the barriers of time and space, creating a profound harmony among all creatures in the universe.

In Arcturian consciousness, love is seen as a vibrant and powerful energy that flows freely, without restrictions or judgments. It is an unconditional love, devoid of expectations or limitations, that embraces all creation. The Arcturians invite us to open our hearts to this unconditional love, allowing it to manifest in our lives and interactions with others.

Beyond love, unity is an essential principle in the Arcturian worldview. The Arcturians recognize that all forms of life are interconnected and that we are part of a greater whole. They understand that separation and division are illusions of the human mind and that, in reality, we are all interconnected aspects of universal consciousness.

In Arcturian consciousness, unity is valued and cultivated as a state of expanded awareness. The Arcturians encourage us to transcend the boundaries of duality and recognize the interconnectedness of all things. By embracing unity, we can overcome superficial differences and unite in a common purpose of spiritual evolution and cosmic harmony.

These extraordinary beings invite us to remember our divine nature and the intrinsic connection we share. They teach us that by acting from love and unity, we can overcome conflicts, heal wounds, and create a reality based on compassion, cooperation, and mutual respect.

Arcturian consciousness reminds us that the pursuit of love and unity begins internally. Through self-love and acceptance of our divine essence, we become channels for radiating love and fostering unity around us. The Arcturians encourage us to nurture and cultivate a loving relationship with ourselves, recognizing our own light and intrinsic value.

As we open ourselves to the principles of Arcturian consciousness, we are invited to transform our lives and co-create a new reality in tune with love and unity. The Arcturians are here to guide us on this journey, reminding us of our divine nature and empowering us to live a life filled with love, compassion, and harmony.

# 5
# The Arcturian Frequency

Now, we delve into the theme of the Arcturian frequency and how attuning to this higher energy can transform our life experience.

The Arcturian frequency refers to the specific energetic vibration associated with the Arcturians and their expanded consciousness. This frequency resonates at a higher octave, transcending the limitations of the three-dimensional reality in which we are immersed. By connecting with the Arcturian frequency, we open doors to higher consciousness and greater alignment with our divine self.

The Arcturians are masters of working with energy and frequency. They understand that everything in the universe is composed of vibrational energy and that we can influence our reality by consciously manipulating this energy. By harmonizing our vibration with the Arcturian frequency, we become channels for higher energy, allowing it to flow through us and deeply transform our lives.

One way to attune to the Arcturian frequency is through meditation. By calming the mind and opening ourselves to the present experience, we can connect with the subtle energies that permeate the universe. The Arcturians invite us to cultivate moments of stillness and contemplation, allowing the Arcturian frequency to envelop and elevate us to states of expanded consciousness.

In addition to meditation, intention and conscious visualization (techniques explained later in the book) are powerful tools for attuning to the Arcturian frequency. By directing our intention and imagination, we can create an energetic field around us that resonates with the Arcturian vibration. Visualizing oneself bathed in bluish light, the color associated with the Arcturians, can strengthen this connection and open channels to Arcturian wisdom and healing.

Music and sound also play a significant role in attuning to the Arcturian frequency. The Arcturians deeply understand the influence of sound and vibration on human consciousness. Listening to music or frequencies that resonate with Arcturian energy can elevate our vibration and deepen our connection with their consciousness.

It is important to note that, from the Arcturian perspective, the "Arcturian frequency" does not refer to a specific sound frequency in terms of Hertz. Instead, it is an expression that represents a state of consciousness and vibrational energy associated with the Arcturians and higher dimensions of existence. However, certain sound frequencies, like the 528 Hz Solfeggio frequency, often linked to DNA repair and transformation, can assist in achieving elevated states of consciousness.

Attuning to the Arcturian frequency is not merely an external technique. It is an invitation to cultivate higher states of consciousness in our daily lives. This involves becoming aware of our thoughts, words, and actions, seeking to align them with the energy of love, unity, and compassion. By living in coherence with Arcturian principles, we align with the flow of the universe and awaken our own cosmic consciousness.

# 6
# Guardians of Peace

The Arcturians are known as masters of peace and harmony. Their society is based on principles of cooperation, compassion, and mutual respect. They deeply understand the interconnectedness of all beings and the importance of living in harmony with one another and the cosmos.

As guardians of peace, the Arcturians play a vital role in maintaining energetic balance throughout the universe. They collaborate with other stellar civilizations to promote peace, stability, and spiritual evolution in various planetary systems.

One way the Arcturians contribute to universal harmony is through the transmission of healing energy and light. They can channel high-vibrational cosmic energies, directing them to individuals and places most in need. This healing energy works on physical, emotional, and spiritual levels, restoring balance and promoting inner and outer harmony.

Moreover, the Arcturians are exceptional mediators and facilitators of conflict resolution. They possess a profound understanding of interdimensional dynamics and can work subtly to resolve disputes and foster reconciliation. Their approach is rooted in compassion, empathy, and the pursuit of solutions that benefit all involved.

Another important aspect of the Arcturians' role as peacekeepers is their work as spiritual mentors. They share their ancestral wisdom and assist other civilizations in expanding their consciousness and awakening to their true nature. By offering teachings and practices, the Arcturians encourage spiritual evolution on both individual and collective levels.

Additionally, the Arcturians participate in planetary healing projects. They collaborate with other stellar races to restore ecological and energetic balance to planets, aiding in the healing of wounds caused by wars, environmental destruction, and energetic imbalances. Their approach emphasizes collective consciousness and the understanding that all beings are interconnected.

The Arcturians inspire us to take responsibility for our inner peace and contribute to peace in the world around us. They remind us that peace begins within ourselves and radiates outward. By cultivating peace and harmony in our own lives, we help create a more peaceful and balanced society.

As guardians of peace, the Arcturians work tirelessly to promote stability, healing, and spiritual growth across planetary systems. Their role as healers, mediators, spiritual teachers, and planetary caretakers reflects their dedication to advancing and maintaining peace in the cosmos.

As we progress on our journey toward enlightenment, we can learn much from the Arcturians and incorporate their principles of peace, love, and harmony into our lives. By doing so, we become co-creators of a more peaceful and harmonious world, aligned with the Arcturians' mission to guide humanity toward enlightenment.

# 7
# Spiritual Evolution

The Arcturians possess ancestral wisdom that spans eras and dimensions. This wisdom encompasses various aspects of existence, from the nature of consciousness to the secrets of the universe. They have a profound understanding of universal laws and cosmic forces that govern the functioning of reality.

One of the fundamental teachings of the Arcturians is the importance of unconditional love. They remind us that love is the essence of the universe and the force that connects all things. Unconditional love transcends the ego and allows us to see beyond superficial differences, recognizing the unity underlying everything that exists. By practicing unconditional love, we expand our consciousness and align with the divine essence within us all.

In addition, the Arcturians teach us the importance of self-transformation and the constant pursuit of spiritual evolution. They encourage us to explore our inner world, question our beliefs and limiting patterns, and seek a deeper understanding of ourselves and the purpose of our existence. Through self-reflection and spiritual practices, we can expand our consciousness and awaken to our true nature.

Another teaching of the Arcturians is the realization that we are multidimensional beings. They remind us that our existence transcends physical reality and that we have access to higher dimensions of consciousness. Embracing our multidimensional nature allows us to explore different aspects of ourselves, unlock latent knowledge and abilities, and expand our perception of reality.

The Arcturians also emphasize the importance of connecting with nature and the universe. They remind us that we are an integral part of the cosmic fabric and that nature reflects our own essence. Reconnecting with nature and honoring its wisdom nurtures our connection to the whole and strengthens our bond with the universe.

Another central aspect of Arcturian teachings is the practice of meditation and inner stillness. They invite us to turn inward, quiet the mind, and access expanded states of consciousness. Through meditation, we can connect with our intuition, tap into subtle knowledge and information, and experience a profound sense of peace and connection with the divine.

The teachings of the Arcturians serve as a source of inspiration and guidance for those seeking spiritual evolution. They invite us to elevate our consciousness, practice unconditional love, explore our multidimensional nature, and cultivate a deep connection with the universe. By integrating these teachings into our spiritual journey, we can expand our awareness, awaken to our true nature, and contribute to the positive transformation of the world around us.

# 8
# Signs, Symbols, and Channeling

As we explore the world of the Arcturians and their wisdom, the question arises of how we can communicate with these powerful cosmic entities. The Arcturians have a unique way of connecting with us, using signs, symbols, and even channeling to convey messages and guidance.

Communication with the Arcturians often begins with noticing signs and synchronicities in our daily lives. These signs can manifest in various forms, such as repeated numerical sequences, unexpected encounters, vivid dream patterns, or even messages that seem to appear out of nowhere. These signs act as calls from the Arcturians, reminding us of their presence and inviting us to pay attention.

In addition to signs, the Arcturians also communicate through symbols. These symbols may appear during meditations, dreams, or even in everyday situations. Each symbol holds a unique and personal meaning, resonating with the individual receiving the message. Trusting our intuition when interpreting these symbols is essential, as they can reveal valuable information about our spiritual journey and life purpose.

Another method of communication with the Arcturians is the practice of channeling. Channeling involves opening oneself to receive messages and information directly from the Arcturians or higher entities. It can be done through automatic writing, trance speech, or even telepathic communication. Channeling requires a deep connection with our inner self and a state of receptivity to allow the messages to flow through us. It is important to practice discernment when receiving channeled messages and seek to validate their authenticity through our intuition and judgment.

Moreover, the Arcturians invite us to develop subtler and more intuitive communication with them. This can be achieved through regular meditation, inner stillness, and self-connection practices. By quieting the mind and opening the heart, we can establish a deeper connection with the Arcturians and receive intuitive guidance in our lives.

It is crucial to emphasize that communication with the Arcturians is an individual and personal experience. Each person may have a unique way of connecting with them, and there is no right or wrong approach. The key is to cultivate an open mind, trust our intuition, and remain willing to receive the messages and guidance the Arcturians offer.

As we open ourselves to communication with the Arcturians, we can receive profound insights, clarifying guidance, and a sense of loving support. This communication reminds us that we are connected to a vast and benevolent universe that is always guiding us on our spiritual journey.

# 9
# Cosmic Healing

The Arcturians are known as powerful agents of cosmic healing, capable of assisting in the process of transformation and energetic balance on profound levels. Their connection to universal energy and elevated consciousness grants them extraordinary healing abilities that can be directed for the benefit of humanity.

One way the Arcturians act as agents of transformation is through energy healing. They can detect and work with the subtle energy fields of the human body, identifying blockages, imbalances, and dysfunctional patterns. With their understanding of cosmic energy and ability to manipulate it, the Arcturians can channel healing energies to dissolve blockages, restore healthy energy flow, and promote holistic healing.

Additionally, the Arcturians provide emotional and spiritual support during the healing process. They are present as compassionate and loving guides, ready to help us understand the emotional roots of our imbalances and overcome past traumas. Their loving and nurturing energy envelops us in a healing energetic embrace, providing comfort, clarity, and insights that allow us to release limiting patterns and move towards wholeness.

A powerful tool the Arcturians use for cosmic healing is sacred geometry. They understand the proportions and geometric patterns that form the universe's foundation, which can be used to realign and restructure energy on subtle levels. The Arcturians employ these sacred geometric forms to create healing chambers, where energy is transformed and recalibrated to promote holistic healing.

Cosmic healing performed by the Arcturians is not limited to the individual but also encompasses collective and planetary levels. They collaborate with other cosmic entities and beings of light to bring healing and balance to humanity's collective consciousness. Their goal is to elevate the planet's vibration, assist in healing ancient wounds, awaken consciousness, and guide humanity towards its spiritual evolution.

It is essential to note that the Arcturians' cosmic healing transcends the physical, emotional, and spiritual planes, reaching the mental realm as well. They work harmoniously with the human mind, helping to restructure limiting thought patterns, negative beliefs, and conditioning that prevent us from accessing our highest potential. With their assistance, we can unlock harmful mental patterns, expand our consciousness, and awaken to a new understanding of the universe and ourselves.

The Arcturians are powerful agents of transformation, bringing cosmic healing to individuals, humanity, and the planet as a whole. Their ability to work with energy, sacred geometry, and elevated consciousness places them in a unique position to assist us on our path to healing, spiritual growth, and evolution. By connecting with the energy of the Arcturians and embracing their loving assistance, we can create space for deep healing, transformation, and the manifestation of our true potential as divine beings journeying through this vast and mysterious universe.

# 10
# Astral Travel and Dimensional Encounters

The Arcturian experience is a fascinating journey beyond the limits of known reality, where individuals have the opportunity to explore astral travels and dimensional encounters. The Arcturians are masters in this art, inviting us to expand our consciousness and explore realms beyond ordinary perception.

Astral travel involves experiences where the consciousness temporarily separates from the physical body to journey into other dimensions or planes of existence. During these travels, we can explore spiritual realms, interact with beings from other spheres, and access profound knowledge and insights.

The Arcturians are skilled guides in these astral journeys, offering us direction and protection during our explorations. They teach us techniques for astral projection, helping us develop the ability to temporarily release the limits of the physical body and explore realms beyond the veil of ordinary reality.

During these astral journeys, we may encounter Arcturian beings and other beings of light inhabiting these realms. Dimensional encounters with the Arcturians can be incredibly enriching, as they share their wisdom and love with us, helping to expand our consciousness and awaken us to our true multidimensional nature.

These dimensional encounters also deepen our understanding of ourselves and our purpose on Earth. The Arcturians help us remember our cosmic origins and guide us in integrating these cosmic truths into our human experience. They encourage us to embrace our divine nature and incorporate this awareness into our daily lives, acting as beacons of light in a world often obscured by illusion.

During astral travels and dimensional encounters with the Arcturians, we may also receive activations and downloads of information to aid in our spiritual evolution. These transmissions of energy and knowledge are tailored to our individual needs, accelerating our growth and awakening.

It is worth noting that the Arcturian experience is not limited to individual astral travels. There are also healing chambers and learning spaces aboard Arcturian ships where individuals can connect with the Arcturians on a deeper level. These encounters may occur in a meditative state or during sleep, allowing the Arcturians to work on our energy field, provide healing, and transmit valuable teachings and insights.

Upon returning from these Arcturian experiences, we may feel transformed and inspired on our spiritual path. Astral travels and dimensional encounters with the Arcturians help us expand our consciousness, remember our cosmic connection, and awaken to the vastness of the universe beyond what our physical senses can perceive.

Each Arcturian experience is unique and personal. What is experienced during these journeys is deeply individual and can vary from person to person. However, the essence of these experiences is the connection with the Arcturians and the expansion of consciousness toward a broader reality.

As we venture into astral travels and dimensional encounters with the Arcturians, we are invited to leave behind the limits of the mind and embrace the vastness of the cosmos. It is an opportunity to explore, learn, heal, and grow on levels beyond what we can imagine. These experiences invite us to transcend the known and open ourselves to the magic and mystery of the universe.

# 11
# The Ascension of Consciousness

The ascension of consciousness is a profound and transformative process currently taking place on our planet. It is a collective awakening to a new reality—an expansion of consciousness inviting us to transcend the limitations of daily life and reconnect with our true divine nature.

As we progress on our spiritual paths, many of us are experiencing significant shifts in our consciousness. We are becoming more aware of our connection to the whole, the universe, and all forms of life. A deep resonance with the fundamental principles of love, compassion, unity, and respect for all beings is emerging.

The ascension of consciousness invites us to release old beliefs and limiting patterns that no longer serve us. We are being called to let go of social conditioning, fears, and illusions that have kept us imprisoned in a limited reality. By shedding these old structures, we create space for a new understanding and experience of life.

A central aspect of the ascension of consciousness is the expansion of perception and understanding of reality. We are becoming aware of planes of existence beyond the physical world, subtle dimensions where energy and consciousness manifest in different ways. These higher dimensions are filled with beings of light, spiritual guides, and benevolent energies ready to support us on our journey.

As our consciousness rises, we are also experiencing changes in our bodies and energy. We are becoming more sensitive to subtle energies around us and learning to navigate this new field of expanded consciousness. Many of us are awakening to spiritual abilities and gifts, such as heightened intuition, healing capabilities, and telepathic connection.

However, the ascension of consciousness is not only an individual process; it is also a collective transformation affecting all of us as a society and species. As more and more people awaken to their true nature, old systems and structures misaligned with this new consciousness begin to disintegrate. We are witnessing significant changes in areas such as politics, economy, environment, and human relations as we move toward a more balanced and harmonious society.

The ascension of consciousness invites us to recognize and honor our interconnectedness with all forms of life. We are learning to live in harmony with the Earth and take responsibility for our role as stewards of this planet. We are awakening to the understanding that we are all part of an interconnected web of energy and consciousness, and our individual actions have a collective impact.

As we continue to elevate our consciousness, we are called to integrate these experiences and understandings into our daily lives. The ascension of consciousness is not just about having elevated spiritual experiences but about living an authentic and meaningful life. It is about bringing this new consciousness into our relationships, work, community, and all areas of existence.

As we move forward on this journey of ascension, we are supported by cosmic beings such as the Arcturians, who are here to guide us and remind us of our true potential as beings of light. They remind us that we are co-creators of our reality and have the power to manifest a new and beautiful way of living.

# 12
# Unlocking Divine Potential

At the core of our existence lies a complex structure of genetic information known as DNA. Traditionally, DNA has been understood as the foundation of our biological inheritance, transmitting physical traits from one generation to the next. However, beyond its biological function, DNA contains an untapped divine potential—a matrix of cosmic knowledge and wisdom waiting to be unlocked.

According to Arcturian concepts, DNA activation is a process involving the expansion of consciousness and the awakening of dormant parts of our genetic information. This activation occurs through our conscious intention and the reception of cosmic light frequencies and information.

To begin the DNA activation process, it is essential to be open and receptive to inner transformation. We can start by setting a clear intention to reconnect with our divine essence and unlock our latent potential.

The Arcturians guide us in meditations and energetic practices to tune into higher vibrations and access the divine codes within our DNA. Meditation is a powerful tool for calming the mind, creating space to connect with our inner essence, and allowing cosmic energy to flow within us. During meditation, we can visualize our DNA being bathed in pure and vibrant light, imagining what it would be like to live fully aligned with our divine potential.

Another technique that can be explored for DNA activation and consciousness expansion is the practice of conscious breathing or sacred breathing. This technique has been used for millennia in various spiritual traditions and possesses the power to connect us with our deepest selves and universal energy.

Conscious breathing involves directing our attention to the breath and bringing full awareness to the process of inhaling and exhaling. It invites us to become present in the moment and connect with the life force flowing through us.

During conscious breathing practice, sensations, insights, or internal experiences often arise. It is important to remain open to these experiences, allowing them to unfold naturally without judgment or expectations. Each person may have a unique experience during conscious breathing, and it is crucial to respect and honor their personal journey.

Conscious breathing is a powerful tool for DNA activation and consciousness expansion, helping us tune into the divine wisdom and power residing within. This practice can be performed regularly, either as part of a longer meditation or as an independent technique to bring clarity, calm, and inner connection.

To complement the practice of conscious breathing and enhance the reception of light frequencies and cosmic information, meditation can be used as an effective technique. Meditation is a powerful means to calm the mind, open up to spiritual connection, and tune into cosmic energies.

By practicing meditation regularly, you strengthen your ability to align with light frequencies and cosmic information. Over time, you may notice increased mental clarity, profound insights, intuitive perceptions, and deeper connections with your divine essence and the universe.

# 13
# Tools for Transformation

The Arcturians are renowned for their advanced knowledge and use of cutting-edge technologies that support spiritual evolution and personal transformation. Their technological tools are designed to elevate consciousness, harmonize energies, and aid in healing and spiritual growth.

One of the main technologies utilized by the Arcturians is vibrational frequency technology. They understand that everything in the universe consists of energy vibrating at different frequencies. Through their advanced devices, they can adjust and balance the energetic frequencies within our auric field.

These devices can detect blockages, distortions, and imbalances in our energy fields and work to realign and restore harmony. They operate on subtle levels, penetrating our physical, emotional, and energetic bodies to dissolve negative patterns and activate the potential for healing.

Additionally, Arcturian technology includes intention-amplification devices. These advanced tools help strengthen our focus and intention, allowing us to manifest our desires and goals more effectively. They empower us to become conscious masters of our reality, using the power of the mind and intention to create positive changes in our lives and the world around us.

Another significant tool employed by the Arcturians is cellular regeneration technology. Recognizing that our cells have the capacity for renewal and rejuvenation, the Arcturians have developed advanced methods to accelerate this regenerative process. These methods can be applied to heal diseases, repair injuries, and promote rejuvenation and longevity.

Beyond physical tools, the Arcturians also utilize subtle energetic technologies, such as the channeling of light and sound frequencies. They transmit specific energies through encoded light and sound frequencies directed toward an individual's energy field. These frequencies act as keys to unlock portals of consciousness, expand perception, and awaken latent aspects of higher awareness.

The Arcturians generously share their advanced technology with those ready to receive and integrate these frequencies and tools into their spiritual journey. However, they emphasize the importance of inner development and emotional balance as foundational elements for fully utilizing these technologies. They remind us that technology is an extension of our consciousness, and we must cultivate a state of clarity, pure intention, and unconditional love to maximize its benefits.

As we explore and open ourselves to Arcturian technology, we are invited to expand our horizons and connect with the vastness of the universe. These advanced tools help us transcend limitations, heal old wounds, and access our divine potential. By incorporating these technologies into our spiritual practices and daily lives, we pave the way for deep and lasting transformation.

# 14
# Star Children

Humanity is composed of unique individuals, each carrying a distinctive story and essence. Among these souls are those known as "Star Children," special beings whose origins trace back to the distant stars of Arcturus.

Star Children are souls who chose to incarnate on Earth with a deep connection to the Arcturians. They carry unique wisdom and energy intended to assist in spiritual evolution and the awakening of collective consciousness. These souls have a profound affinity with Arcturian energy and exhibit distinct characteristics that set them apart from others.

One of the primary traits of Star Children is heightened sensitivity and compassion. They possess a deep empathy for other beings and feel an intrinsic connection to all life. This compassion is accompanied by an inner wisdom and an understanding of the universe's deeper truths. From an early age, these children may demonstrate an uncommon grasp of life's mysteries and a relentless quest for meaning.

In addition, Star Children have enhanced intuitive and psychic abilities. They naturally access information and subtle energies beyond the reach of physical senses. These children may exhibit gifts such as clairvoyance, telepathy, energy healing, and even astral travel. Their connection with the Arcturians allows them to serve as channels of communication between dimensions and realities.

However, it's crucial to recognize that when a Star Child doesn't find their path, they may feel lost and face difficulties in various areas of life. They may experience a sense of incompleteness and lack purpose, feeling disconnected from their Arcturian origins. If you identify with this sense of incompleteness, it's possible that you are one of these Star Children seeking your path. When the energies that naturally harmonize your life are not properly directed, it can lead to disharmony in your existence.

Discovering your Arcturian origin and opening yourself to this connection is essential for flourishing in all aspects of life. By diving into this journey of self-discovery and embracing your cosmic origins, you create space for Arcturian energies to flow into your life. As this connection strengthens, you'll experience a sense of fulfillment and inner alignment. In this state, every area of life harmonizes, leading to living in abundance, happiness, and harmony.

It's time to open yourself to the possibility that you are one of these Star Children searching for your path. By reconnecting with your Arcturian origins, you allow these energies to flow freely, unlocking inner wisdom and triggering significant transformations. As you align with your cosmic essence, you'll find greater prosperity, love, and health because everything is interconnected in the grand tapestry of the universe.

Embrace your Arcturian nature and allow yourself to flourish as the Star Child you are. May your journey of self-discovery and connection with your cosmic origins be filled with light, love, and achievements in every area of your life. You are a precious part of the cosmos, and by embracing your Arcturian essence, you'll discover the power and completeness that have always resided within you.

# 15
# The Expansion of Consciousness

The expansion of consciousness is an incredible and transformative process that invites us to explore the boundaries of our understanding and integrate Arcturian energies into our evolutionary journey. As we embark on this path, we are encouraged to broaden our worldview, raise our vibration, and reconnect with our true essence.

The Arcturians, as beings of light and wisdom, are our guides on this journey of expanding consciousness. They are ready to support our spiritual growth by offering profound knowledge and healing energies that help us awaken to a new understanding of reality.

One of the first steps to integrating Arcturian energies into our consciousness is to develop a regular meditation practice. Through meditation, we can calm the mind, open our hearts, and tune into the subtle frequencies of the Arcturians. In this state of inner stillness, we can receive insights, guidance, and even experiences of contact with these elevated beings.

As we advance in our journey of expanding consciousness, it is essential to cultivate authenticity and a connection to our essence. The Arcturians remind us that we are multidimensional beings with a divine heritage. They encourage us to explore our gifts, talents, and passions and express them fully in the world. Aligning with our inner truth creates space for integrating Arcturian energies into our being.

A fundamental aspect of expanding consciousness is emotional and energetic healing. As we open ourselves to Arcturian energies, we are invited to release old limiting patterns, negative beliefs, and emotional traumas. The Arcturians stand beside us, offering their love and light to assist in this deep healing process. We can call upon their presence and ask for their assistance in letting go of everything that no longer serves us.

By integrating Arcturian energies, we begin to experience a broader consciousness and heightened sensitivity and intuition. We access knowledge and wisdom beyond the rational mind, connecting to a higher awareness. This Arcturian wisdom invites us to live by elevated principles such as unconditional love, compassion, respect for life, and harmony with nature.

As we delve deeper into the integration of Arcturian energies, we are called to share our experiences and wisdom with others. We can become channels of light and love, radiating these energies into the world around us. The Arcturians encourage us to act as emissaries of their message of unity, healing, and transformation, inspiring others to awaken to their inner divinity.

# 16
# Intergalactic Collaboration

As we expand our consciousness and explore the universe's depths, we discover that we are not alone. A vast intergalactic network of beings of light and wisdom is ready to collaborate with us on our evolutionary journey. In this chapter, we delve into the concept of intergalactic collaboration and how it can help us advance on our path of spiritual growth.

The Arcturians, as an advanced stellar race, understand the importance of intergalactic collaboration. They recognize that evolution is not limited to a single race or planet but is a collective effort spanning the entire cosmos. They have worked closely with other galactic civilizations, exchanging knowledge, experiences, and energies to accelerate the process of planetary ascension.

One form of intergalactic collaboration is the sharing of advanced technology. Stellar civilizations have developed technologies beyond our current comprehension, including interdimensional travel, energy healing, and telepathic communication. By establishing connections with these intergalactic races, we gain the opportunity to receive and integrate these technologies into our journey.

Moreover, intergalactic collaboration involves the exchange of spiritual knowledge and teachings. Each civilization has its ancestral wisdom, healing methods, and spiritual practices that can enrich and expand our understanding of the universe and ourselves. The Arcturians, in particular, possess a profound comprehension of universal principles of love, unity, and cosmic connection. By connecting with them, we can access these universal truths and apply them to our spiritual path.

Intergalactic collaboration also occurs on an energetic level. Stellar civilizations constantly communicate and exchange elevated energies. By tuning into these energies, we can strengthen our connection with the divine and accelerate our awakening process. We can invoke the presence of the Arcturians and other stellar races to receive their blessings and energetic activations, paving the way for a more rapid and harmonious evolution.

It is important to emphasize that intergalactic collaboration is based on equality, respect, and mutual cooperation. It is not about dependency on more advanced stellar races but a balanced exchange of knowledge and energies. Each human being has a unique contribution to offer in this grand cosmic evolution project, and through collaboration, we can unite and advance toward a future of peace, love, and expanded consciousness.

Intergalactic collaboration reminds us of the vastness of the universe and our potential to connect with it. By opening ourselves to connections with beings from other galaxies, we expand our vision of the cosmos and tap into an ocean of cosmic wisdom and love. This collaboration allows us to progress more rapidly on our spiritual journey, bringing benefits not only to ourselves but to all humanity and the universe itself.

# 17
# Accessing Higher Dimensions

Stellar portals are connection points between different regions of the universe, enabling transit between various dimensions and planes of existence. They are like bridges leading us to realities beyond what our physical senses can perceive. The Arcturians understand the importance of these portals as gateways to spiritual growth and the expansion of consciousness.

By aligning our energy with the Arcturians' frequency and opening ourselves to the possibility of accessing stellar portals, we can connect to higher levels of consciousness and cosmic wisdom. These portals function as energy channels, allowing us to receive downloads of information, insights, and transcendental experiences.

To access a stellar portal, it is necessary to raise our vibration and attune our energy to the frequency of higher dimensions. The Arcturians are specialists in this field and can guide us on this journey of exploring stellar portals.

Crossing through a stellar portal transports us to a reality beyond our current comprehension. We may experience visions, encounters with beings of light, access to advanced knowledge, and an expansion of our senses and perceptions. These experiences allow us to break free from the confines of three-dimensional reality and connect with a broader universal consciousness.

It is essential to remember that stellar portals are not just entry points but also exits. As we explore higher dimensions and receive teachings and energies from these realms, we have the responsibility to bring this wisdom back to our three-dimensional world. We must integrate and anchor these experiences into our daily lives, sharing them with others and contributing to the collective elevation of consciousness.

I invite you to reflect on the existence of stellar portals and the possibility of accessing higher dimensions. The Arcturians encourage us to explore these portals with humility, curiosity, and respect, understanding that we are multidimensional beings with the potential to connect to a vast universe of knowledge and wisdom.

# 18
# Restoring Energetic Balance

Let us delve into the fascinating role of the Arcturians as cosmic healers, exploring their abilities and techniques to restore energetic balance on individual, planetary, and universal levels. The Arcturians are known for their profound understanding of subtle energies and their ability to transmute and harmonize discordant patterns.

The Arcturians understand that health and well-being are intrinsically linked to the state of energetic balance. They recognize that all illnesses and imbalances stem from misalignments and blockages in the energies flowing through the physical, emotional, mental, and spiritual bodies. Thus, their healing approach is holistic, encompassing all aspects of being.

One of the primary techniques used by the Arcturians is energy transmutation. They can channel and direct high-frequency energy to dissolve negative and unbalanced patterns. This healing energy acts as a "purifying light," dissolving blockages and restoring the natural flow of energy.

In addition to energy transmutation, the Arcturians are masters in utilizing sacred geometry and healing symbols. They understand that certain forms and geometric patterns possess specific healing properties and can be used to restore energetic balance on subtle levels. These symbols act as keys that unlock access to higher states of consciousness where healing becomes possible.

Another crucial aspect of Arcturian healing is working with consciousness. The Arcturians believe true healing does not occur solely on the physical level but also at the level of awareness. They assist individuals in expanding their consciousness, releasing limiting patterns, and awakening to their true essence. In doing so, they create an environment conducive to healing and transformation on all levels.

The Arcturians also collaborate with other beings of light and cosmic healers to bring restoration and healing to planetary and universal systems. They are part of a vast network of intergalactic healers united in missions of transformation and healing, working to elevate the vibration of planets, galaxies, and beyond.

The Arcturians invite us to open our hearts and minds to receive their healing assistance, whether through direct connection or by applying the principles and techniques they share. By embracing their wisdom, we can restore energetic balance within ourselves and contribute to the broader harmony of the universe.

# 19
# Planetary Consciousness

The Arcturians invite us to expand our perception and recognize that we are part of an interconnected whole, where every being and element on the planet plays a vital role.

Planetary consciousness refers to the understanding that Earth is a living organism, pulsating with its own energy and consciousness. It is interconnected with all forms of life inhabiting it, including humans. The Arcturians teach us that by tuning into the Earth's consciousness, we can nurture a harmonious and co-creative relationship with our planetary home.

One way to connect with Earth's consciousness is through the practice of meditation and grounding. By quieting our minds and focusing our attention on Earth's heart, we can establish a profound connection with its energy and wisdom. This connection enables us to access insights and guidance directly from Earth itself, guiding us on our individual and collective journeys.

The Arcturians remind us that by connecting with Earth's consciousness, we also awaken our responsibility as stewards of the planet. They encourage us to adopt a conscious and sustainable lifestyle, honoring natural resources and acting in harmony with nature's cycles. By doing so, we contribute to the healing and regeneration of our home and all forms of life that inhabit it.

Additionally, the Arcturians emphasize the importance of uniting as a global community for Earth's well-being. They encourage us to overcome divisions and differences, recognizing that we are all part of one human family. When we unite in love and compassion, we can co-create a world of peace, balance, and harmony.

By exploring planetary consciousness and joining with Earth's heart, we become agents of change and transformation. The connection with Earth's consciousness inspires us to act for environmental preservation, social justice, and the elevation of collective awareness.

It is essential to deeply understand that our connection to Earth goes beyond physical and material relations. It is an energetic and spiritual connection that reminds us of our interdependence with all beings and the planet as a whole. By uniting with Earth's heart, we pave the way for personal and collective transformation.

# 20
# Ancient Knowledge

Let us delve into the vast repository of ancestral wisdom of the Arcturians. This wisdom transcends time and connects us to ancient knowledge that can assist us in our journey of spiritual awakening and personal evolution. The Arcturians invite us to remember and access this knowledge, deeply rooted in our collective consciousness.

The ancestral wisdom of the Arcturians encompasses various aspects of existence, from universal principles to spiritual practices and advanced technologies. This wisdom is familiar to us on a profound level, even if we do not consciously recall it. As we open ourselves to connecting with the Arcturians and attune our consciousness to theirs, we can access dormant knowledge.

One area where the ancestral wisdom of the Arcturians stands out is their understanding of the universe's fundamental principles. They teach us about the primordial energy that permeates everything and how we can work consciously with this energy to create our reality. These principles include the law of attraction, conscious manifestation, and co-creation with the universe.

Additionally, the Arcturians share advanced spiritual practices that support our evolutionary process. They teach us the importance of meditation, visualization, and connecting with our divine essence. These practices help us expand our consciousness, access higher planes of existence, and align with our life's purpose.

The Arcturians also possess deep knowledge about the subtle energies of the body and the human energy field. They teach techniques for energy healing and chakra balancing, enabling us to restore harmony and health on all levels of our being. These techniques allow us to release blockages, elevate our vibration, and awaken our inner healing potential.

Furthermore, the ancestral wisdom of the Arcturians includes scientific and technological insights. They have advanced knowledge in areas such as free energy, interdimensional travel, and telepathic communication. While we may not immediately master these abilities, we can draw inspiration from them and begin exploring these fields with an open and curious mind.

As we delve deeper into the Arcturians' ancestral wisdom, we become aware that this ancient knowledge is available to us. We can access it through our intuition, meditation, and connection with the Arcturians as guides and mentors. By opening ourselves to this wisdom, we can integrate it into our daily lives, bringing greater clarity, purpose, and expanded consciousness.

# 21
# Vibrational Transformation

Vibrational transformation refers to the change in our energetic state and frequency of vibration. As we open ourselves to the understanding that we are vibrational beings, we begin to perceive the influence our energy has on our reality. The Arcturians teach us that raising our vibration is essential to access higher planes of existence and experience a deeper connection with our divine essence.

One key to vibrational transformation is becoming aware of and purifying our patterns of thought, emotions, and behavior. The Arcturians invite us to carefully examine our minds and hearts, identifying limiting beliefs, fears, and traumas that may prevent us from vibrating at higher frequencies. By releasing these dense energies, we create space for expansion and the elevation of our vibration.

Another fundamental aspect of vibrational transformation is the regular practice of self-care and energy-enhancing techniques. The Arcturians offer us various tools, such as meditation, conscious breathing, creative visualization, and working with light, to help raise our frequency. These practices assist in balancing our energy centers, expanding our consciousness, and aligning us with the higher frequencies of love, compassion, and gratitude.

Additionally, the Arcturians emphasize the importance of nurturing our physical, emotional, and spiritual well-being. Healthy eating, appropriate physical exercise, contact with nature, and moments of tranquility are essential to maintaining an elevated vibration. By caring for our entire being, we align our energies and allow our inner light to shine brightly.

As we commit to vibrational transformation, we begin to experience significant changes in our lives. Our relationships become more harmonious, our intuition deepens, and we attract positive and abundant experiences. We also become clearer channels for divine energy, allowing it to flow through us and positively impact the world around us.

It is essential to understand that vibrational transformation is a continuous process. As we evolve, we are constantly invited to raise our vibration and expand our consciousness. The Arcturians are always present to support us on this journey, offering loving guidance and reminding us of our unlimited potential.

# 22
# Unity in the Multiverse

Duality is an intrinsic part of the human experience. We live in a world of opposites, where there is light and darkness, joy and sorrow, love and fear. Duality challenges us to find balance and harmony within ourselves and in our interactions with the world around us. The Arcturians teach us that true transformation occurs when we embrace and integrate these opposites, discovering the unity that underlies them.

The journey of integrating duality begins with the awareness and acceptance that we are multidimensional beings. The Arcturians invite us to expand our consciousness beyond the limitations of the three-dimensional reality and recognize the many facets of our being. They remind us that every aspect of ourselves, both light and shadow, plays a vital role in our growth and evolution.

As we explore our inner duality, the Arcturians encourage us to embrace our shadow and heal it with compassion and love. Recognizing and integrating our fears, traumas, and less desirable aspects allows us to achieve greater inner unity. By embracing all parts of ourselves, we become more authentic and complete beings.

Furthermore, the Arcturians invite us to transcend polarity in our relationships and interactions with others. They remind us that every person we encounter is a mirror of ourselves, reflecting our own dualities. By seeking to understand and accept others, regardless of differences, we pave the way for unity and genuine connection.

Throughout this journey of integration, the Arcturians highlight the importance of non-judgment. They encourage us to release the need to label experiences as good or bad and instead adopt a broader and more compassionate perspective. By doing so, we can see beyond superficial appearances and recognize the divinity present in all forms of life.

The Arcturians also remind us that unity is not limited to our planet but extends to the entire multiverse. They invite us to connect with cosmic consciousness and understand that we are part of a vast web of interconnected energy. As we open ourselves to this expanded awareness, we can access information and wisdom from other dimensions and cosmic beings.

Unity is the foundation of transformation and ascension. By embracing our duality, transcending polarity, and connecting with the oneness of the multiverse, we align ourselves with higher consciousness and the infinite potential of creation.

# 23
# Spiritual Path

The Arcturians are enlightened beings who possess a deep understanding of higher dimensions and are ready to assist us on our spiritual journey. Known for their wisdom and compassion, they have the ability to connect deeply with our spiritual essence and understand the challenges and obstacles we encounter along the way. As spiritual mentors, they offer guidance and loving support, helping us navigate life's complexities and

One of the primary ways the Arcturians guide us is through channeling and telepathic communication. They establish an energetic bond with us, allowing us to receive messages and insights directly from them. These communications can come in the form of words, images, feelings, or intuitions, helping us expand our awareness and understanding.

In addition, the Arcturians guide us in developing our intuition and connection with our inner wisdom. They encourage us to trust our inner voice, feelings, and ability to discern the truth. They remind us that each of us has a divine spark capable of guiding us towards our unique journey.

The Arcturians show us how to access universal healing energies and assist us in transforming and transcending emotional, mental, and spiritual challenges we may face. With their loving guidance, we are encouraged to let go of the past and fully embrace our potential for growth and transformation.

Furthermore, the Arcturians teach us the importance of authenticity and the full expression of who we are. They encourage us to be true to ourselves, honoring our unique gifts and talents. They remind us that each of us plays a vital role in collective awakening and that, by embracing our authenticity, we contribute to the evolution of global consciousness.

Throughout our spiritual journey, the Arcturians remind us that we are always surrounded by unconditional love and divine support. They encourage us to nurture a continuous connection with the spiritual presence and trust their guidance. They help us remember that we are powerful and creative beings capable of manifesting a reality aligned with our highest essence.

As we deepen our relationship with the Arcturians as spiritual mentors, we are invited to cultivate a regular practice of meditation, introspection, and connection with nature. These practices help us strengthen our connection with the spiritual realm and receive clarity and insights on our journey.

As we progress in this book, we recognize profound gratitude for the teachings and guidance of the Arcturians. They are our loving and compassionate allies, always available to support us in our spiritual quest. By integrating their teachings and incorporating their guidance, we become more aligned with our true essence and open the doors to a life of greater love, wisdom, and enlightenment.

# 24
# Healing and Transforming

Unconditional love is a vibrant energy that flows from the divine heart. It is a love that expects nothing in return, does not judge, transcends the limitations of the ego, and embraces the wholeness of who we are. When we open ourselves to receiving and expressing this love, we can heal old wounds, transcend separation, and reconnect with our divine essence.

The Arcturians are masters in cultivating and expressing unconditional love. They show us that love is the essence of our being and that, by opening our hearts, we can become channels for this divine energy. They encourage us to practice unconditional love in our daily lives, beginning with deeply and completely loving ourselves.

When we love ourselves unconditionally, we free ourselves from limiting beliefs and patterns of self-sabotage. We recognize our own divinity and intrinsic worth, regardless of our perceived flaws or imperfections. This self-compassion and acceptance are fundamental to our inner healing and transformation.

Moreover, the Arcturians remind us that unconditional love extends beyond ourselves and embraces all of humanity. They invite us to extend this love by practicing compassion, empathy, and generosity. By cultivating relationships based on unconditional love, we can build a global community of support, healing, and mutual growth.

One way we can express unconditional love is through forgiveness. The Arcturians teach that forgiveness is a powerful tool for healing, as it frees us from the burden of resentment, bitterness, and hurt. By forgiving others and ourselves, we create space for healing and transformation to occur in our lives.

Unconditional love also invites us to recognize the interconnectedness of all life and to act in harmony with collective well-being. The Arcturians show us that every thought, word, and action rooted in love has a positive impact on the whole. They inspire us to contribute to the elevation of collective consciousness and the creation of a more loving and compassionate world.

As we deepen our practice of unconditional love, we experience profound inner transformation. Our hearts expand, our relationships become more meaningful, and we become agents of positive change in our communities and the world.

Through the practice of this divine love, we can heal old wounds, transcend separation, and reconnect with our true nature. The Arcturians are loving guides on this journey, reminding us of the power of love and encouraging us to express it in all areas of our lives.

# 25
# Attracting Aligned Experiences

Arcturian resonance refers to the vibrational attunement to the energy and consciousness of the Arcturians. As we open ourselves to this resonance, we connect with the higher frequencies of love, wisdom, and healing that the Arcturians represent. This connection enables us to align our intentions and create a life that reflects our true essence.

The Arcturians are beings of light with a profound understanding of universal laws and energy. Their purpose is to assist in the spiritual evolution of humanity and the expansion of planetary consciousness. Their loving and wise presence guides us to connect with our divine essence and awaken to a higher level of consciousness.

One way to create Arcturian resonance is through meditation and the regular practice of connecting with Arcturian energy. During meditation, we can visualize and feel the presence of the Arcturians around us, surrounding us with their light and love. As we open ourselves to this connection, we allow their elevated energies to merge with ours, raising our vibration and expanding our awareness.

During this meditative experience, we can also connect with the cosmic wisdom and knowledge of the Arcturians. They are masters in advanced technology, energy healing, and consciousness expansion. By attuning to their resonance, we can access insights and guidance that aid us on our journey.

The Arcturians also teach us the importance of working with energy and intention. They show us that we are co-creators of our reality and that we can attract experiences aligned with our vibration and intention. When we attune to Arcturian resonance, we activate our personal power and become aware of how our choices and energies shape our reality.

In addition to meditation, Arcturian resonance can also be cultivated through conscious intention and alignment with Arcturian principles. The Arcturians encourage us to live according to the values of unconditional love, compassion, harmony, and service to the greater good. By incorporating these principles into our daily lives, we attract experiences and opportunities aligned with our spiritual evolution.

As we create Arcturian resonance in our lives, we also connect with the energy of the whole. We are part of an interconnected universe, and by raising our vibration, we contribute to the collective elevation of consciousness. Our individual experiences intertwine with humanity's journey as a whole, and each step toward expanding our awareness is a gift to collective growth.

# 26
# Collective Consciousness

We now arrive at a crucial point in our journey: the awakening of collective consciousness and the emergence of a new paradigm in society.

Collective consciousness refers to the sum of all individual consciousnesses that make up humanity. It is the energetic field that connects us to one another and influences the interactions and experiences we share as a species. For many centuries, collective consciousness has been dominated by fear, separation, and limitation.

However, we are witnessing a collective awakening, a movement toward a new paradigm based on love, unity, and an understanding of the interconnectedness of all things. This awakening is driven by an increase in spiritual awareness, the awakening of souls, and the desire for a higher, more harmonious reality.

As more individuals awaken to their true spiritual nature, they begin to realize they are not separate from one another or the greater whole. This realization leads to a transformation in how we relate to and interact with the world around us. Individualism gives way to compassion, cooperation, and the pursuit of the common good.

The awakening of collective consciousness also invites us to question the existing structures and systems in our society. As we recognize the interconnectedness of all things, it becomes evident that approaches based on competition, exploitation, and inequality are unsustainable in the long term.

In this new paradigm, we seek to create a society based on collaboration, mutual respect, and care for the planet. We value diversity and inclusion, recognizing that every individual has a unique role to play in the web of life. Together, we work to find creative solutions to global challenges, prioritizing sustainability, social justice, and the well-being of all beings.

As collective consciousness continues to expand, new forms of social, economic, and political organization emerge. We are witnessing the rise of conscious communities, grassroots movements, and increased citizen participation in decision-making. Technology also plays a crucial role, connecting people from different parts of the world and facilitating the sharing of information and ideas.

This awakening of collective consciousness does not happen overnight but is a continuous and evolutionary process. It requires each of us to do our part, both individually and collectively. We need to be willing to examine our own beliefs and thought patterns, letting go of what no longer serves us and embracing a mindset of expansion and growth.

By awakening collective consciousness and embracing a new paradigm, we are creating a brighter and more sustainable future for generations to come. Each of us has a vital role in this transformation, as we are all interconnected, and our individual actions have a collective impact.

# 27
# Conscious Manifestation

In the pursuit of creating the desired reality, the energy of intention plays a crucial role. Intention is a powerful force that directs our energy and guides our actions. Let us now delve into the importance of focusing our intention clearly and purposefully to manifest our deepest desires.

Intention is the starting point for conscious manifestation. It is the result of a process of self-exploration and self-discovery, where we connect with our true desires and purposes. By identifying and clarifying our intentions, we are setting the direction we want to follow and establishing a solid foundation for conscious creation.

A clear intention is like a compass that guides us on our manifestation journey. When we have a clear vision of what we wish to create, our thoughts, emotions, and actions align harmoniously with that goal. The clarity of intention helps us focus our energy, channeling it effectively toward the realization of our desires.

A powerful way to strengthen our intention is to visualize the desired outcome in vivid detail and with emotion. Creative visualization is a practice that allows us to experience in advance the reality we wish to manifest. By vividly imagining what it would feel like to achieve our goal, we activate the energy of intention and amplify its creative power.

Moreover, it is essential to maintain the intention consistently over time. The energy of intention requires perseverance and commitment. By staying focused on our desires and believing in their realization, we keep the flame of conscious manifestation alive. Regularly reaffirming and reminding ourselves of our intentions strengthens our connection to the universe's creative energy.

Another fundamental aspect of the energy of intention is trust. It is necessary to trust in our ability to manifest what we desire. Trust is a driving force that propels our intention forward, overcoming obstacles and doubts that may arise along the way. By believing in our capacity to create the desired reality, we activate the creative power within us.

The energy of intention also benefits from a mindset of gratitude. By expressing gratitude in advance for the fulfillment of our intentions, we strengthen the connection with the energy of manifestation. Gratitude is a powerful magnet that attracts more things to be grateful for.

Cultivating a gratitude mindset opens space for the abundant flow of creative energy in our lives. The energy of intention is amplified when combined with inspired action. Intention alone is not enough; we must act in alignment with our desires. Inspired action arises from a place of connection with our intuition and leads us to opportunities and synchronicities that support us on our manifestation journey. By acting in alignment with our intentions, we actively co-create our desired reality.

Every thought, emotion, and action carries a unique energetic vibration. The energy we emit into the universe acts as a magnet that attracts experiences and circumstances resonating with that vibration. Thus, if we wish to manifest a positive reality aligned with our dreams and desires, it is essential to elevate our vibration and tune into a frequency compatible with what we want to attract.

A fundamental practice for harmonizing our vibrations is meditation. Meditation helps us calm the mind, quiet our thoughts, and connect with our inner self. Through meditation, we can enter a state of deep relaxation and open space for higher energy to flow through us. Regular meditation helps us elevate our vibration and tune into more positive frequencies.

In addition to meditation, creative visualization is a powerful tool for aligning our vibration with the desired frequency. By clearly and vividly visualizing the reality we wish to manifest, we send a clear message to the universe about what we want to attract. By imagining in detail what it would be like to experience that desired reality, we align our vibration with the frequency of that manifestation.

Positive affirmations also play a significant role in harmonizing vibrations. By repeating positive affirmations related to our desires and goals, we reprogram our mind and strengthen a mindset of abundance and positivity. These affirmations help elevate our vibration, replacing limiting thought patterns with empowering beliefs.

Gratitude is a powerful practice that helps us raise our vibration. By expressing gratitude for what we already have in our lives, we activate the energy of love and appreciation. Gratitude places us in a state of abundance, allowing our vibration to rise and attract more things to be grateful for. Cultivating a gratitude mindset opens space for positive experiences and conscious manifestation.

Another way to harmonize our vibrations is by taking care of our physical body. Eating healthily, exercising, resting adequately, and nurturing emotional well-being are essential aspects of raising our vibration. When our body is in balance and harmony, our energy flows freely, enabling us to tune into higher frequencies.

Music and sound also have the power to influence our vibration. Certain musical frequencies, such as classical, meditative music, or nature sounds, have a calming and vibration-raising effect. By listening to and appreciating these types of music, we tune our vibration to harmony and serenity, aiding in conscious manifestation.

It is important to remember that each of us has the power to raise our vibration and tune into the desired frequency. Through practices such as meditation, visualization, positive affirmations, gratitude, self-care, and exposure to high frequencies, we can create a vibrational field that attracts experiences and manifests our deepest desires.

# 28
# Journey of the Soul

Within each of us resides a divine spark, a cosmic essence that transcends earthly existence. At the core of our being, we can sense an inner calling, a gentle voice inviting us to reconnect with our Arcturian essence. Let us explore the awakening of this calling and the journey of reconnection with our true stellar identity.

Often, the inner calling manifests as a feeling of longing or nostalgia, a profound sense that we belong to a place beyond this world. As we open ourselves to listen to this call, we begin to notice synchronicities in our lives, serendipitous encounters, and a series of events that guide us toward our Arcturian essence.

Reconnecting with the Arcturian essence is a personal and unique process for each individual. It begins with the awakening of consciousness, the realization that there is more than what our physical senses can perceive. As we expand our awareness, we can access deep knowledge and insights about our stellar origin.

During this journey of reconnection, it is essential to open ourselves to intuition and trust the messages we receive. Intuition is the language of the spirit, an inner compass guiding us toward our true essence. By honoring and following our intuition, we are led to situations, people, and opportunities that help us connect with our Arcturian nature.

Furthermore, the practice of meditation plays a fundamental role in reconnecting with the Arcturian essence. Through meditation, we can calm the mind and create space for communication with our Arcturian guides and mentors. In these moments of stillness, we may receive insights, visions, and messages that help us remember who we are and our mission on this earthly plane.

As we reconnect with the Arcturian essence, we begin to awaken unique abilities and gifts that have lain dormant within us. These abilities may include energy healing, telepathy, channeling, clairvoyance, and more. Each individual possesses specific talents that are integral to their Arcturian nature.

Throughout this journey of reconnection, it is important to cultivate self-love and compassion. Challenges and questions may arise as we reconnect with our essence, but it is crucial to remember that we are on a path of growth and expansion, and every step is valuable. Self-love helps us overcome doubts and fears, nurturing a deeper connection with our essence.

As we explore the inner calling and reconnect with the Arcturian essence, we create space for profound transformation in our lives. We feel a renewed sense of purpose and clarity about our spiritual path. Recognizing and honoring the Arcturian nature is an embrace of uniqueness, contributing to the evolution of collective consciousness.

In the depths of our consciousness lie ancestral memories of our Arcturian origin. These cosmic memories remain dormant, patiently waiting to be awakened.

As we open ourselves to the possibility of a connection with the Arcturians, we begin to perceive subtle hints and signs in our daily lives. These signs may appear as vivid dreams, visions, intuitions, or a deep sense of familiarity with the stars. They guide us toward the memories of our existence beyond this earthly plane.

During the exploration of our Arcturian origins, we may encounter visions of stellar landscapes, advanced technologies, and harmonious interactions with beings of light. These images can bring feelings of nostalgia and a profound longing to return to our cosmic home. It is important to remember that these memories are a valuable part of our spiritual journey and can help us understand our purpose here on Earth.

As we delve deeper into the exploration of our Arcturian origins, we may also connect with spiritual guides and mentors who assist us on this journey of awakening. These beings of light possess deep knowledge of Arcturian energies and can offer guidance, support, and healing throughout the process. Establishing a connection with these guides opens doors to a deeper understanding of our cosmic identity.

Exploring our Arcturian origins also leads us to recognize and embrace our innate gifts and abilities. These talents may range from energy healing to channeling, telepathic abilities, intuitive wisdom, and more. Reconnecting with our Arcturian essence makes these gifts more accessible, enabling us to use them for personal and collective well-being.

It is essential to note that the awakening of cosmic memories can be a gradual and unique process for each individual. There is no fixed timeline or rigid expectations. Every step taken toward these memories is valuable and contributes to our spiritual evolution.

As we dive into the exploration of our Arcturian origins and awaken cosmic memories, we are invited to embrace our true essence and share our knowledge and experiences with the world. These memories empower us to play a significant role in the transformation of collective consciousness and the creation of a more harmonious world.

# 29
# Unification of Consciousness

Within the fabric of existence, we are all interconnected through a powerful web of collective consciousness. Every thought, emotion, and action reverberates through this invisible web, creating an impact that extends far beyond ourselves.

Collective consciousness refers to the idea that all human beings are energetically interconnected, forming a complex network of relationships and influences. Each of us acts as a node in this web, contributing to collective consciousness through our experiences, beliefs, and intentions. When we become aware of this interconnectedness, we can begin to perceive the profound impact our choices have on the whole.

By recognizing this web of interconnectedness, we become responsible not only for our own lives but also for the health and well-being of the collective. Our energies intertwine and influence one another, creating a powerful synergy that can be directed toward building a world of peace. Every act of kindness, compassion, and love we perform reverberates through the collective consciousness, positively affecting those around us and beyond.

Unity lies at the heart of collective consciousness. When we recognize that we are all part of a greater whole, we let go of the artificial divisions we create and seek collaboration and mutual understanding. We realize that our differences are complementary, and together, we can embrace diversity and build an inclusive and harmonious world.

One of the most powerful ways to strengthen collective consciousness is through group meditation or the creation of spaces for connection and sharing. When we gather in a state of presence and conscious intention, our energies align and amplify, generating a powerful wave of harmony that spreads through the collective field. These practices also allow us to access expanded states of consciousness, where we can receive insights and inspirations that serve the greater good.

Moreover, education plays a fundamental role in building collective consciousness. By promoting mutual understanding, empathy, and appreciation of diversity from a young age, we prepare future generations to embrace unity and peace. Learning extends beyond formal classrooms and can take place in various environments, such as communities, organizations, and families.

As we become aware of our connection to collective consciousness, we can collaborate to address the challenges we face as humanity. Together, we can co-create creative and sustainable solutions for social, environmental, and economic issues. We believe in the collective strength and the power of unity to overcome divisions and promote peace at all levels.

In the depths of our existence, ancestral memories echo from the stars. As we connect with our Arcturian essence, we awaken the cosmic memories that link us to divine origins. Cosmic memories are fragments of knowledge and experiences that transcend our current existence. By awakening these memories, we begin to unravel the deepest layers of our identity and understand our purpose in this vast universe.

Exploring Arcturian origins opens doors to a cosmic perspective of our existence. Immersing ourselves in our Arcturian heritage invites us to embody these qualities in our earthly journey.

As we awaken cosmic memories, we begin to recognize patterns in our lives aligned with Arcturian energy. We may feel a deep connection with healing, advanced technology, inner peace, and the pursuit of spiritual knowledge. These are intrinsic aspects of our Arcturian nature that can be cultivated and incorporated into our journey.

One way to explore our Arcturian origins is through meditation and deep dives into our inner world. By quieting the mind and opening the heart, we connect with the ancestral wisdom flowing through us, receiving insights, guidance, and memories that help us understand our connection to the Arcturians and how to bring their energy into our daily reality.

Additionally, studying Arcturian culture and philosophy can provide valuable insights into our origins. Listening to channeled teachings and messages from Arcturian beings may resonate deeply with our soul, further awakening the cosmic memories within us.

As we explore our Arcturian origins, it is essential to remain open and receptive to the experiences and signs that emerge along our path. Attuning to this energy, we may notice synchronicities, significant encounters, and opportunities for spiritual growth that guide us further along our journey.

Remembering our Arcturian essence is an invitation to live in alignment with the wisdom, love, and peace that characterize this energy. It is a call to unite as a collective consciousness, co-creating a world of peace and harmony. Awakening cosmic memories and connecting with our Arcturian essence contributes to the unification of consciousness and the manifestation of a bright future for all humanity.

# 30
# Spiritual Mastery

On the path to spiritual mastery and the development of Arcturian potential, a fundamental aspect is awakening cosmic consciousness and exploring higher dimensions. These dimensions transcend physical reality and offer a vast field of knowledge, wisdom, and consciousness expansion. Let us explore the various facets of these higher dimensions and the importance of awakening this cosmic consciousness on our journey of spiritual expansion.

Higher dimensions are realms of elevated vibrational consciousness, where time, space, and the limitations of physical reality differ from what we are accustomed to. These dimensions are inhabited by beings of light, spiritual guides, and cosmic beings of wisdom and unconditional love. By accessing these dimensions, we can expand our awareness and connect with a deeper understanding of the universe and our divine purpose.

The awakening of cosmic consciousness invites us to transcend the limitations of the egoic mind and perception, opening ourselves to a broader vision of existence. When we become aware of the higher dimensions and attuned to their energy, we gain access to a vast reservoir of wisdom, healing, and spiritual guidance. This cosmic consciousness enables us to remember our connection to the universe and understand that we are multidimensional beings on an evolutionary journey.

By exploring higher dimensions, we can employ different practices and techniques to expand our awareness. Meditation is a powerful tool for achieving altered states of consciousness and opening portals to higher dimensions. Creative visualizations, breathing techniques, and the use of crystals can also serve as aids in this process of exploration.

During these experiences, we may encounter spiritual guides, ascended masters, and cosmic beings who are available to guide us on our spiritual journey. They may impart teachings, offer healing, and help us awaken our inner Arcturian potential.

By awakening cosmic consciousness and exploring higher dimensions, we are gifted with a series of benefits. Access to profound spiritual wisdom, greater mental clarity, expanded intuition, and emotional and spiritual healing are just a few examples. Furthermore, this connection allows us to co-create our reality in a way that is more aligned with our divine essence, manifesting a life of purpose, abundance, and love.

As we explore higher dimensions and awaken our cosmic consciousness, we open the doors to a vast universe of possibilities. Connecting with these dimensions takes us on a journey of self-discovery and spiritual expansion, enabling us to access our inner Arcturian potential. By cultivating this cosmic consciousness, we find greater harmony, inner peace, and a deeper connection with the fabric of the universe. We are ready to explore higher dimensions and embrace our true cosmic nature.

On the path to spiritual mastery and the expansion of Arcturian potential, engaging in self-transformation practices is essential for developing and enhancing our Arcturian abilities. These abilities are rooted in our true cosmic selves and can be accessed and cultivated through specific practices. Let us explore some of these practices and techniques that allow us to expand our awareness and awaken our Arcturian abilities.

Self-transformation practices are fundamental to spiritual development and the expansion of our Arcturian abilities. They help us release limiting patterns, negative beliefs, and dense emotions, allowing energy to flow freely within our being. Additionally, these practices connect us to inner wisdom, awaken our intuition, and strengthen our connection to higher realms of consciousness.

Arcturian Meditation:

Arcturian meditation is a powerful practice that enables us to attune to Arcturian energy and frequency. During this meditation, we can visualize Arcturian light bathing our entire being, purifying us, and activating our energy centers. This practice helps align our vibration with that of the Arcturians, opening us to the guidance and wisdom they offer.

Arcturian DNA Activation:

Arcturian DNA activation is a process of reactivating the light codes and information present in our DNA related to our cosmic Arcturian heritage. This practice involves visualizations, affirmations, and intentions to awaken and activate these latent codes, allowing our awareness to expand and our Arcturian abilities to manifest.

Arcturian Energy Work:

Working with Arcturian energy involves the conscious and intentional use of Arcturian cosmic energy for healing, transmutation, and manifestation. This practice may include techniques such as laying on of hands, visualizing Arcturian light flowing through the body, and connecting with Arcturian beings for guidance and assistance in energy work.

Multidimensional Consciousness Expansion:

Developing Arcturian abilities involves expanding our awareness beyond the physical dimension and contacting different levels of multidimensional existence. Techniques such as meditation, visualization, and breathing exercises can be used to open portals of consciousness and explore higher realms of existence. This practice enables us to access our cosmic wisdom, connect with our spiritual guides, and expand our understanding of reality.

Self-transformation practices are valuable tools for developing and enhancing our Arcturian abilities and connecting with our cosmic essence. By engaging in these practices, we open the doors to a journey of spiritual growth and expanded consciousness. As we awaken our Arcturian abilities, we become channels of light and love, contributing to the creation of a world of peace and harmony.

# 31
# Cosmic Purpose

Within every human being lies a cosmic purpose, a unique and special mission intrinsically connected to the energy and consciousness of the Arcturians. This chapter presents the journey of awakening to cosmic purpose and the recognition of the Arcturian mission on Earth.

The Arcturian awakening journey is a path of self-discovery, consciousness expansion, and connection with Arcturian energy. It is an invitation to explore and develop our latent spiritual capacities, expand our perception, and awaken to the greater purpose of our lives.

The first step on the Arcturian awakening journey is to look within and embark on a path of deep self-knowledge. Self-knowledge is essential, as it allows us to understand who we truly are beyond the superficial layers of personality and external influences. It is a journey to discover our true essence and recognize our connection to the universe and the Arcturians.

Reflection on Life Experiences:

Regularly taking time to reflect on your life experiences is a powerful practice. This involves observing your actions, relationships, successes, and challenges, and conducting an honest analysis of how you react to them. This deep reflection enables a better understanding of your motivations, fears, desires, and behavioral patterns.

Questioning Beliefs:

By questioning your beliefs, you challenge ideas that prevent you from reaching your highest potential. Often, these beliefs are internalized over time based on past experiences or external influences. Asking whether these beliefs are truly valid and beneficial creates space for new perspectives and possibilities.

Exploring Talents and Passions:

Exploring your talents and passions is another crucial aspect of self-knowledge. Ask yourself: What brings me joy? What am I good at? What inspires and makes me feel alive? Identifying these areas aligns you more closely with your cosmic purpose and the Arcturian energy.

Meditation and Introspection:

Meditation and introspection are powerful tools for connecting with your inner essence and creating space for spiritual awakening. Meditation allows you to calm the mind, cultivate mindfulness, and deepen your connection with yourself and the divine. Dedicate daily time to sit in silence, focus on your breathing, and observe the thoughts and emotions that arise. As you refine your meditation practice, you will access deeper levels of awareness and contact your true nature.

In addition to meditation, introspection involves investigating your own mind and heart. This can be done through self-questioning, journaling, or discussing your ideas and experiences with a spiritual mentor or support group. Introspection enables you to delve into the deeper layers of your being, uncover unconscious patterns, and discover new insights and understandings.

Recognize that we all have shadow aspects and emotional wounds, and that part of the journey is embracing these parts of ourselves with compassion. Acceptance and forgiveness are fundamental to releasing the past and moving forward toward spiritual awakening.

As you deepen your self-knowledge and connect with your inner essence, you open the doors to Arcturian awakening. This journey of self-discovery and consciousness expansion is a solid foundation for embarking on a path of connection with the Arcturians and discovering the cosmic purpose intrinsically tied to your existence.

# 32
# Expansion of Consciousness

The expansion of consciousness is an essential aspect of the Arcturian awakening journey. As we open ourselves beyond the boundaries of physical reality, we can explore higher dimensions of existence and connect with Arcturian energy and wisdom. Below, we explore some ways to expand your consciousness on this journey:

Explore different spiritual belief systems. There are numerous spiritual traditions worldwide, each with its own perspectives on human existence and the cosmos. By opening yourself to different belief systems, you broaden your understanding of the world and spiritual possibilities. Read sacred texts, study ancient philosophies, and research diverse religions and spiritual practices. In doing so, you can extract valuable knowledge that resonates with your own journey.

Beyond religious belief systems, there is a vast range of philosophies and spiritual teachings to explore. These philosophies may address profound existential questions and provide insights into the nature of consciousness and reality. Study the teachings of philosophers, spiritual masters, and contemporary thinkers who offer inspiring perspectives and stimulate your inner quest.

Reading inspiring books is a powerful way to expand consciousness. Seek out works that address topics such as spirituality, consciousness expansion, metaphysics, cosmology, quantum physics, and transpersonal psychology. Renowned authors in these fields, such as Deepak Chopra, Eckhart Tolle, Rupert Spira, and Gregg Braden, can provide insights and knowledge to awaken your understanding and awareness.

Remain open and receptive to new perspectives and ideas. Be willing to question your own beliefs and preconceptions. Sometimes, the expansion of consciousness involves challenging and transcending limitations imposed by society, culture, and conventional education. Be willing to explore new horizons and consider new possibilities to pave the way for Arcturian wisdom.

# 33
# Energetic Harmonization

Energetic harmonization is a fundamental component of the Arcturian awakening journey. The Arcturians work with subtle and vibrational energies, and attuning to their energy requires the harmonization of the physical, emotional, and spiritual bodies. Let's explore some techniques and therapeutic modalities that can help in this process:

Reiki is an energy healing technique that involves channeling universal energy through the hands to promote balance and healing. Reiki practitioners use sacred symbols and hand positions to direct energy to areas of the body that need harmonization. This practice helps release energetic blockages, revitalize the body, and align with Arcturian energy.

Crystals have unique energetic properties and can be used as tools for harmonization. Each crystal has a specific vibration that resonates with certain aspects of our being. By using crystals in meditation, placing them on chakras, or positioning them around the body, we can balance and amplify energies, facilitating energy flow and promoting harmonization. The choice of crystals can be based on personal intuition or knowledge of each stone's specific properties.

Beyond the techniques mentioned above, various other therapeutic modalities can contribute to energetic harmonization. Examples include acupuncture, energy massage, sound therapy, aromatherapy, and guided meditation. Each modality addresses energy in different ways, offering alternative paths to balance and harmonize the physical, emotional, and spiritual bodies.

When practicing energetic harmonization techniques, it is important to remain present and open to receiving energy, allowing it to flow through you. Be conscious of your own sensations and responses during practices, as each person may have a unique experience. As you release blockages, balance your chakras, and align with Arcturian energy of love and healing, you create an energetic field conducive to the awakening journey and connection with the Arcturians.

# 34
# Multidimensional Abilities

Let's explore the importance of recognizing and accepting your multidimensional gifts. Each of us possesses unique abilities that go beyond the five physical senses, and acknowledging these gifts is the first step toward awakening and developing your maximum potential.

To begin, reflect on how you feel about your intuitive and perceptive abilities. Often, people may experience an inner knowing, intuition that guides them, or synchronicities in their lives. These are signs that you have multidimensional gifts ready to be explored.

It is essential to let go of any doubts or limiting beliefs that may be blocking your recognition of these gifts. We are often conditioned to believe that abilities beyond the "normal" are not real or valid. However, by opening yourself to the possibility that you can access higher levels of consciousness, you expand your boundaries and allow your gifts to manifest.

During this recognition process, pay attention to recurring signs and patterns in your life. Notice the areas where you excel, where your intuition is particularly strong, or where you feel naturally drawn. These are indications of specific gifts waiting to be acknowledged and cultivated.

Additionally, be open to exploring different modalities for expressing your multidimensional abilities. Not everyone has the same gifts or abilities, and this diversity makes each of us unique. Some may excel in energy healing, while others may have an innate capacity to channel spiritual messages or interpret symbols.

Be willing to experiment and discover which modality resonates most with you. Seeking guidance from spiritual mentors, attending workshops or courses on developing multidimensional abilities, or dedicating yourself to practices of self-exploration and inner connection can be helpful.

Remember that recognizing and accepting your multidimensional gifts is a continuous process. As you progress on your spiritual journey, new gifts may emerge, and others may deepen. Stay open to possibilities and embrace your true multidimensional nature.

As we awaken our multidimensional gifts, we can access these dimensions and expand our consciousness beyond the limits of three-dimensional reality.

Higher dimensions are realms of consciousness where energy is more subtle and vibrant. In these planes, we can experience greater freedom, clarity, and connection with our divine essence. It is a space where we can reconnect with our true Self and access information, wisdom, and spiritual guidance.

To explore higher dimensions, it is essential to be open and receptive to this possibility. Often, the rational mind resists what cannot be tangibly proven, but remember that reality is much more vast and complex than our physical senses can capture.

A way to begin exploring higher dimensions is through meditation. Meditation helps calm the mind and create space for expanded awareness. By entering a meditative state, we can raise our vibration and attune to higher energy frequencies.

During meditation, direct your intention to connect with higher realms and allow spiritual information and experiences to unfold. Stay open to insights, visions, sensations, or messages that may arise. Trust your intuition and let your awareness expand beyond physical reality.

Exploring higher dimensions requires balance and discernment. It is essential to remain grounded and care for your physical and emotional well-being while venturing into these higher spheres. Stay connected to

Earth, nurture your body, and practice self-care to sustain a healthy and harmonious experience.

As you become familiar with and explore higher dimensions, you expand your understanding of reality and your connection to the universe as a whole. This exploration can bring greater clarity about your purpose and mission on Earth, allowing you to be a channel of light and love for your benefit and that of all humanity.

Each of us has unique and innate abilities, and through continuous practice and development, we can refine and use them for the greater good. Here are some suggestions to help you develop and enhance your multidimensional abilities:

Awareness and Self-Knowledge: Before developing your abilities, it is important to have a clear understanding of your capacities and gifts. Conduct self-examination to identify the areas where you feel naturally connected and talented. This self-awareness will guide your development efforts.

Education and Study: Seek resources and information about the abilities you wish to develop. Books, courses, workshops, and mentors are excellent ways to learn specific techniques and gain expert guidance. Be open to continuous learning and expanding your knowledge.

Regular Practice: Like any skill, multidimensional development requires regular practice. Dedicate time to exercising and honing your abilities. Whether telepathy, clairvoyance, energy healing, or any other capacity, practice them consistently to strengthen and build confidence.

Meditation and Inner Attunement: Meditation plays a fundamental role in developing multidimensional abilities. It calms the mind and allows access to higher states of consciousness. Use meditation to connect with your intuition, receive guidance, and expand your perception beyond physical limits.

Group Work and Community: Join groups or communities of like-minded individuals. Participating in collective practices, such as group meditations or developmental exercises, can strengthen your abilities and provide enriching exchanges of experiences. Collaboration with others can also offer support and encouragement along the way.

Integrity and Ethics: When developing your abilities, always act with integrity and ethics. Use your gifts for the greater good, respecting and obtaining consent from those involved. Be responsible and aware of the impact of your actions, using your abilities to promote love, healing, and personal growth.

As you develop and refine your multidimensional abilities, you expand your capacity to be an agent of positive transformation in the world. Remember that this development is an ongoing and individual journey. Be patient with yourself, trust your process, and remain open to discovering and exploring new facets of your unlimited potential.

As you develop and refine your abilities, the responsibility arises to use them for the benefit of all and to advance collective consciousness. Sharing your gifts is a powerful way to contribute to humanity's positive transformation. Consider the following when sharing your gifts with the world:

Authentic Self-Expression: When sharing your gifts, be authentic and true to yourself. Don't try to fit into predefined molds or follow others' expectations. Open yourself to expressing your abilities uniquely and originally, bringing your perspective and contribution to the world.

Identify Your Purpose: Reflect on how your gifts can serve a greater purpose. Ask yourself how your abilities can help elevate collective consciousness, promote healing, inspire creativity, or contribute to harmony and peace in the world. Having clarity about your purpose will allow you to share your gifts more effectively and impactfully.

Find Your Platforms: Discover the best ways to share your gifts with the world. This could include writing books, creating online content, giving lectures, offering workshops, participating in events, or collaborating with other professionals. Find the platforms that resonate with you and enable your gifts to reach a wider audience.

Inspire and Empower Others: Share your gifts with the intention of inspiring and empowering others. Be a beacon of light and wisdom, showing people that they, too, possess unique gifts and potentials. Offer guidance, mentorship, or teachings to help others awaken their abilities and discover their true inner power.

Practice Empathy and Compassion: When sharing your gifts, remember to practice empathy and compassion. Recognize that everyone is on their own path of evolution and respect their pace. Be open to listening to and understanding others' needs, adapting your approach to meet their unique requirements.

Cultivate a Service Mindset: Adopt a mindset of service when sharing your gifts. Be willing to offer your help without expectations or conditions. Recognize the privilege of sharing your gifts and the opportunity to make a difference in others' lives.

Remember that sharing your gifts is not just about giving but also about receiving. As you share your abilities with the world, you also receive inspiration, growth, and learning in return. Be open to mutual exchange and the blessings that arise from this interaction. Share your gifts with love, integrity, and joy, knowing that you are contributing to the manifestation of a more enlightened and conscious world.

# 35
# Galactic Consciousness

As we awaken to our true cosmic nature, we are invited to explore the vast frontiers of the universe and reconnect with the wisdom and mysteries of the cosmos. Here are some reflections to aid you on this journey of expansion:

First, it is important to recognize that you are an integral part of the universe. Just like the stars, planets, and galaxies, you possess a cosmic essence within yourself. Your connection to the universe is intrinsic and profound. Reflect on your stellar heritage and open yourself to understanding that you are a unique and valuable expression of cosmic vastness.

Embracing your connection with the universe requires expanding your consciousness beyond the boundaries of earthly reality. This involves opening up to the idea that there are other dimensions, galactic civilizations, and levels of existence beyond what we can perceive with our physical senses. Explore meditation, contemplation, and inner exploration to expand your consciousness and access new horizons of knowledge and understanding.

To embrace your connection with the universe, it is important to attune yourself to the cosmic frequency. This means developing greater sensitivity to the energies and vibrations of the universe and learning to align with them. Practice inner listening, mindful observation, and connection with nature to enhance your alignment with the cosmic pulse of the universe.

As you deepen your connection with the universe, delve into the search for galactic wisdom. Study ancient cosmic traditions, the teachings of advanced civilizations, and ancestral records that reveal the secrets of the cosmos. Be open to receiving insights, downloads of information, and experiences that lead you to greater knowledge and understanding of the universe and yourself.

Embracing your connection with the universe also involves integrating this awareness into your daily life. It's not just about intellectually understanding the vastness of the cosmos but embodying this awareness in how you live and act in the world. Act with compassion, love, and respect for all forms of life, recognizing that we are all interconnected and part of something greater.

As you become more aware of your connection with the universe, you will recognize your role as a co-creator of reality. You have the power to influence the course of events and shape your destiny. Harness this ability to consciously co-create a reality aligned with your highest vision and purpose, remembering to act in harmony with the cosmic principles of balance, harmony, and love.

As you immerse yourself in the exploration of galactic consciousness and embrace your connection with the universe, allow yourself to be guided by your intuition, heart, and inner curiosity. Celebrate your connection with the cosmos, and let it inspire you to live a full and meaningful life in harmony with the universal energies that permeate all existence.

May this journey through galactic consciousness be a source of discovery, spiritual growth, and expanded awareness of the vastness and beauty of the universe.

# 36
# Reconnection with the Source

When we open ourselves to this profound connection, we are able to remember our true nature and awaken to the greater purpose of our existence. Let us explore some aspects of this process of reconnection:

Recognizing the Inner Divine Presence: The first step in reconnecting with the Source is acknowledging the divine presence within us. Regardless of religious or spiritual beliefs, we all possess a divine spark that connects us to the origin of all that is. Invite this divine presence to manifest in your consciousness, allowing yourself to remember your divine essence and open to the transformative power of unconditional love.

Reconnecting with the Source also involves remembering the unity that permeates all existence. As we awaken to our divine nature, we realize that we are all interconnected and part of a greater whole. This awareness enables us to transcend the illusions of separation and live in harmony with all beings. Meditate on the interconnectedness of all things and allow this awareness to permeate your daily life.

To reconnect with the Source, it is important to cultivate a spiritual practice that resonates with you. This may include meditation, prayer, contemplation, rituals, or any other form of connection with the divine. Dedicate regular time to nurturing your soul and opening to the presence of the Source in your life. As you dive into this practice, you will strengthen your connection with the Source and increasingly remember your divine essence.

As we reconnect with the Source, a process of healing and transformation naturally unfolds in our lives. By remembering our divine essence, we are invited to release limiting patterns, negative beliefs, and emotional wounds that hinder us from fully living our truth. Allow yourself to dive into this process of healing and transformation, seeking support when needed and trusting in the natural flow of life.

Reconnection with the Source also reminds us of our greater purpose in life. As we align with our divine essence, we are guided to live a meaningful life aligned with our unique purpose. Seek within yourself and listen to the gentle voice of your soul, which will guide you toward a life full of meaning, service, and authentic expression of your truth.

Reconnecting with the Source is not an isolated event but an ongoing process of deepening and spiritual growth. As we progress on our journey, it is important to nurture our connection with the Source through regular spiritual practices, moments of stillness, connection with nature, and cultivating relationships and environments that support our spiritual awakening.

As you allow yourself to immerse in reconnection with the Source and remember your divine essence, your life will gain new meaning, purpose, and joy. Let this profound connection with the Source illuminate your path and guide your choices, reminding you that you are a divine being having a human experience. Open yourself to the love and wisdom of the Source, and let it inspire you to live a full, authentic life aligned with your true nature.

# 37
# Arcturian Light

Arcturian Light is an elevated vibrational energy that can be channeled and used to bring healing, transformation, and spiritual awakening. Let us explore some aspects of this energy and how we can radiate it to the world:

Arcturian Light is a pure expression of unconditional love. By radiating this light to the world, you will be sending waves of love and healing to all beings and the Earth itself.

When radiating Arcturian Light, it is important to set a clear and focused intention. You can direct this energy toward specific areas needing healing, such as global conflicts, environmental issues, or even personal situations. Keep your intention clear in your mind and heart as you send Arcturian Light, knowing that your energy is being directed for the greater good of all.

The Arcturian beings are known for their connection to Arcturian Light and are ready to assist us on our spiritual journey. As you radiate Arcturian Light, you may invite their presence and guidance in your healing and service work. Be open to receiving their messages, insights, and assistance as you work with the energy of Arcturian Light.

As you become more familiar with the energy of Arcturian Light, you can expand your capacity to radiate it to the world. This can be achieved through regular meditation and self-care practices, nurturing your inner light and allowing it to shine ever more brightly. As your light expands, you become a beacon of love and healing for others, inspiring and awakening those around you.

By radiating Arcturian Light to the world, you play a significant role in planetary transformation and the elevation of collective consciousness. Remember that you have access to this divine energy and can use it to bring healing, love, and light wherever it is needed. May your journey with Arcturian Light be a profound and transformative experience, allowing you to become an agent of positive change in our world.

# 38
# The Ascension of Humanity

The Arcturian Era and humanity's ascension in consciousness mark a profound shift. The New Era represents a time of great transformation and spiritual awakening, with the teachings and energies of the Arcturians playing a fundamental role in this transition. Let us delve into some aspects of this journey of ascension:

The Arcturian New Era brings a fundamental change in how we view and experience the world. It invites us to transcend a fear-based and limited mindset and embrace an expanded consciousness rooted in love, unity, and the interconnectedness of all things. Humanity's ascension in consciousness involves a radical shift in our belief systems and values as we move toward a more inclusive and holistic vision of reality.

Ascending in consciousness is a process of individual and collective expansion and elevation. As we open ourselves to higher levels of perception, we become aware of higher dimensions and subtle realities previously beyond our understanding. This expansion of consciousness allows us to access information, wisdom, and knowledge that transcend the physical realm, enabling a deeper understanding of ourselves and the universe.

The teachings and energies of the Arcturians play a vital role in humanity's ascension. They offer us guidance, support, and tools to connect with our divine essence, awaken our gifts and potentials, and navigate the changes and challenges of ascension. Integrating these energies involves opening our hearts, raising our vibrations, and embodying the Arcturian principles of love, healing, harmony, and service to the greater good.

As we expand our consciousness, we become aware of our ability to co-create reality. The Arcturian New Era invites us to take responsibility for our experiences and become active agents of change. By aligning our intentions, thoughts, and actions with love and truth, we can manifest a higher reality rooted in harmony, peace, and abundance for all.

The ascension of humanity in consciousness also calls us to embrace unity in diversity. By recognizing and celebrating the variety of cultures, beliefs, and perspectives, we can unite as a global human family. Transcending divisions and separations enables us to build a society based on cooperation, compassion, and mutual respect in harmony with the whole.

As we explore and embrace the Arcturian New Era, we are invited to assume our true divine nature, live in alignment with the Arcturian principles of love, healing, and service, and contribute to humanity's ascension in consciousness. May this chapter inspire you to connect with your own divine essence and play your part in creating a more elevated and conscious world.

# 39
# The Cosmic Unity

As the journey of the Arcturians and their influence reaches its climax, we are invited to explore the nature of universal consciousness and our connection with the whole. Let us delve into some aspects of this awakening:

Universal consciousness refers to the awareness that we are part of an interconnected whole. It is the understanding that everything that exists is interlinked and that each being and element contributes to the fabric of existence. At this stage of our journey, we are called to expand our consciousness beyond individual limits and to recognize the underlying unity that permeates all creation.

Today, we awaken to universal consciousness and realize that we are not separate from the universe but rather a unique and interdependent expression of it. We recognize that every thought, action, and choice we make affects not only ourselves but also the whole. This awareness leads us to take responsibility for our impact on the world and to act with love, compassion, and respect for all forms of life.

As we connect to universal consciousness, we begin to align our lives with the cosmic order. This involves living in harmony with universal principles such as unconditional love, wisdom, truth, and justice. As we tune into these higher energies, we become channels of light and love, radiating these qualities to the world and contributing to the elevation of collective consciousness.

The awakening of universal consciousness also opens us to the possibility of reconnecting with other stellar civilizations. As we expand our perception beyond earthly boundaries, we may sense the presence and influence of other intelligent life forms across the cosmos. This connection reminds us of our cosmic nature and encourages us to cultivate peaceful and collaborative relationships with other civilizations, sharing wisdom and knowledge for mutual benefit.

As we awaken to universal consciousness, we begin to recognize and explore our multidimensional nature. We understand that we exist on different levels of reality and that our consciousness extends beyond the limits of time and space. This understanding empowers us to access and integrate abilities and gifts from other dimensions, enabling us to live a more expansive, creative, and aligned life with our divine essence.

We arrive at the end of this journey recognizing that the awakening of universal consciousness is an invitation to remember who we truly are. We are cosmic beings, connected to the entire universe, with the power to create and shape our reality. As we embrace this truth, we are empowered to live with wisdom, love, and compassion, bringing light and healing to the world around us.

# 40
# Practical Part

Now that we understand the fundamentals and applications of the Arcturian techniques in different aspects, let us proceed to the practical part, where the step-by-step of each technique and the exercises necessary for becoming an Arcturian channel will be explained. It is important to emphasize that, in describing some techniques, the theme may seem repetitive; this is because each technique is described didactically from beginning to end. The combination of techniques enables you to become a channel for Arcturian healing.

# 41
# Channeling

Step 1: Preparation

Find a quiet and comfortable place in your home where you can relax without being interrupted. Make sure you have enough time to dedicate to the practice of channeling.

Cleanse and purify the environment using techniques such as smudging, aromatherapy, or soft music, creating a conducive space for connection.

Be open and receptive, setting aside expectations and judgments. This is a time to explore the connection with the Arcturians with an open mind and a loving heart.

Step 2: Relaxation and Focus

Sit or lie down comfortably. Close your eyes and begin to breathe deeply, paying attention to your breath. Allow your body to relax and release any tension or worry.

Focus on a point of light in the center of your mind, visualizing it as bright and radiant. This will serve as your anchor of concentration during the channeling process.

Step 3: Invocation of the Arcturians

Begin by invoking the presence of the Arcturians. You can do this mentally or aloud, expressing your desire to connect with them and receive guidance, knowledge, and healing.

Be open to receiving the presence of the Arcturians in your consciousness. Feel their loving and peaceful energy around you, ready to communicate with you.

Step 4: Energetic Alignment

Visualize or sense a bright white light descending upon you, enveloping your entire being. Imagine this light filling you with positive and loving energy.

Allow this energy to expand beyond your physical body, connecting with the energy of the Arcturians. Feel unified and in harmony with them, establishing a deep energetic connection.

Step 5: Communication and Channeling

Still in a deep state of relaxation, focus on your anchor of concentration—the point of light in your mind.

Ask clear and specific questions to the Arcturians. You can do this mentally or aloud. Be open to receiving answers through thoughts, words, images, or sensations.

Trust your intuition and allow the messages to flow. Do not worry if they seem like your own thoughts; with practice, you will learn to discern the difference.

Record or write down your experiences, insights, and messages received. This will help you remember and reflect later.

Step 6: Closing and Gratitude

When you feel you have concluded your channeling session, thank the Arcturians for the connection and guidance received.

Slowly bring your awareness back to your surroundings. Gently move your body, stretch, and open your eyes when you are ready.

Record your experiences, insights, and any guidance received. Reflect on what was shared and how it may apply to your personal journey.

# 42
# Automatic Writing

Step 1: Preparation
Find a quiet and comfortable place where you can concentrate without distractions. Ensure you have paper or a notebook and a pen available.

Cleanse and purify the space according to your personal preferences, creating an environment conducive to the practice of automatic writing.

Set aside sufficient time to dedicate to this practice without feeling rushed.

Step 2: Relaxation and Focus
Sit in a comfortable position with your back straight and your feet firmly planted on the floor. Close your eyes and start breathing deeply, allowing your body to relax with each exhalation.

Focus on calming your mind and letting go of any thoughts or worries. Be fully present in the moment, open to receiving the messages that may emerge.

Step 3: Intention and Connection
Set your intention for the automatic writing session. Express your desire to connect with a higher source of wisdom, guidance, or knowledge.

If you prefer, say a brief invocation or prayer to invite the presence of benevolent and loving entities, such as spiritual guides or beings of light.

Step 4: Beginning the Writing

Hold the pen loosely over the paper, keeping your hand relaxed. Start writing without consciously thinking about the content or the words being written.

Let the writing flow freely, without judgment or censorship. Do not worry about spelling, grammar, or sentence structure. The goal is to allow messages to flow spontaneously.

Step 5: Observation State

As you write, observe your mind and inner experience. Be aware of any sensations, emotions, or images that may arise.

Maintain a neutral observer stance, avoiding over-identification with the words being written. Remember that you are channeling information from a source beyond your conscious self.

Step 6: Closing and Reflection

When you feel the automatic writing session is coming to an end, gradually slow your writing until you stop completely.

Read what you have written with an open and curious mind. Highlight or take notes on parts that seem significant, profound, or relevant to you.

Take a moment to reflect on the messages received. Ask yourself what you have learned or how these messages may apply to your life or spiritual journey.

# 43
# Meditation

Step 1: Preparation

Choose a quiet and peaceful place where you can meditate without interruptions. It could be a room in your house, a garden, or any location that provides a calm and relaxing atmosphere.

Sit in a comfortable position, either on a chair with your feet on the floor or on the ground with your legs crossed. Keep your back straight but not rigid, and relax your shoulders.

Step 2: Relaxation

Gently close your eyes and begin breathing deeply. Focus on your breath, observing the air entering and leaving your body. Let your breathing become natural, without forcing it.

Step 3: Breathing Focus

Direct your attention to the sensation of your breath in your body. Observe the movement of air entering and leaving through your nostrils or the rise and fall of your abdomen.

When your mind begins to wander, gently bring your focus back to your breath without judgment or frustration. Simply observe and let the thoughts pass, returning your attention to the breath.

Step 4: Sensory Awareness

As you become familiar with the breath, expand your attention to other senses. Observe physical sensations in your body, such as the feeling of touch in your hands or the sounds around you.

Stay present in the moment, observing sensations, sounds, and your surroundings without clinging to or judging them.

Step 5: Mindfulness Cultivation

As the practice progresses, you can choose to cultivate mindfulness of different aspects, such as present emotions or arising thoughts.

Observe your emotions with curiosity and compassion, allowing them to surface and dissolve. Similarly, observe your thoughts without clinging to them, letting them pass without judgment.

Step 6: Closing

When ready to end the meditation, return your attention to your breath. Feel your body present in the moment and gently open your eyes.

Take a moment to stretch your body, extend yourself, or make gentle movements to bring awareness to your physical surroundings.

Regular meditation practice can bring a range of benefits to the mind, body, and spirit. Starting with short sessions of 5 to 10 minutes a day and gradually increasing the time as you feel comfortable can be an effective approach. Remember that meditation is a personal journey, and each experience can be unique.

The key is to practice consistently and patiently, allowing stillness and calm to permeate your daily life.

# 44
# Visualization

Step 1: Preparation
Find a quiet place where you can concentrate without interruptions. Sit or lie down comfortably in a relaxed position.

Close your eyes and take a few deep breaths to relax your body and calm your mind. Leave behind the day's worries and be present in the moment.

Step 2: Choose a Focus for the Visualization
Determine the goal or intention of your visualization. It could be a goal, an image, or a specific situation you want to create or manifest in your life.

Be clear and specific about what you wish to visualize. The more details you can imagine, the more vivid your experience will be.

Step 3: Create a Mental Scene
Begin to create a mental image of what you wish to visualize. Imagine yourself in this situation or environment with as much detail as possible.

Use all your senses to enrich the visualization. Picture the colors, movements, sounds, smells, and physical sensations associated with your scene.

Step 4: Making the Visualization Vivid
Make the visualization as realistic as possible in your mind. Immerse yourself completely in the

experience as if you were living it in the present moment.

Bring positive and intense emotions to the visualization. Feel the joy, gratitude, confidence, or any other emotion associated with what you are visualizing.

Step 5: Maintaining Focus and Persistence

Stay focused on the visualization, avoiding allowing thoughts or distractions to interfere with your experience.

If your mind begins to wander, gently redirect your focus to the visualization. If necessary, take a deep breath and reorient yourself to the goal of the practice.

Step 6: Closing and Gratitude

When you feel the visualization is complete, express gratitude for the experience and the progress you are making toward your goal.

Slowly open your eyes and return to your surroundings. Take a moment to reflect on the experience and, if desired, jot down any insights or observations in a journal.

Regularly practicing visualization techniques can help strengthen your creative imagination and program your mind to achieve your goals. Remember that visualization is a powerful tool but should also be complemented with practical action in your daily life. With consistency and persistence, visualization can become a powerful ally on your path to manifestation and personal growth.

# 45
# Speaking in Trance

Step 1: Preparation
Find a quiet, distraction-free location where you can fully focus on the practice.
Sit or lie down in a comfortable position that allows relaxation while maintaining alertness.

Step 2: Inducing Trance
Close your eyes and begin relaxing your body through deep, slow breaths. Allow your mind to calm and remain present in the moment.
Visualize a staircase, a serene beach, or any element that helps you relax and enter a trance state.

Step 3: Establishing the Trance
Focus on an idea, concept, or theme you wish to explore during the trance. This could be a question you want to answer or an experience you want to undergo.
Mentally or softly repeat positive affirmations that reinforce your connection to the trance and its purpose.

Step 4: Opening to Channeling
Allow your mind to become receptive to insights, words, or feelings that arise during the trance.
Release any preconceived expectations and be open to receiving information from a higher source of wisdom, whether it is your higher self, spiritual guides, or your subconscious.

Step 5: Verbal Expression

When you feel you are in a trance state, begin to speak softly or whisper the words or phrases that come to your mind.

Do not worry about coherence or logic at this point. Let the words flow naturally, guided by your intuition and insights.

Step 6: Observation and Recording

Pay attention to the words, phrases, or messages that arise during the trance. If possible, record yourself speaking for later review.

At the end of the trance session, take some time to reflect on what was communicated. Write down any insights or observations in a journal for future reference.

Remember that trance and trance-speaking practices require trust, openness, and patience. Each experience may be unique, so allow yourself to explore and adjust the techniques to what works best for you. Over time and with regular practice, you can enhance your ability to communicate deeply and meaningfully during trance states.

# 46
# Telepathic Communication

Step 1: Preparation
Find a quiet environment where you can concentrate without interruptions. Sit or lie down in a comfortable position, keeping your spine straight.

Close your eyes and begin to relax your body and mind through slow, deep breaths. Let go of thoughts and worries, focusing on the present moment.

Step 2: Energetic Tuning
Imagine a bright light filling your entire being, purifying your energy and establishing an internal connection with your higher self.

Visualize your energy channels open and harmonized, ready to receive and transmit telepathic information.

Step 3: Focus on Intention
Set a clear intention for telepathic communication. It could be to contact a spiritual guide, a loved one, or any other being you wish to communicate with telepathically.

Keep this intention in your mind, affirming your openness to communication and establishing a space of love and respect.

Step 4: Mentalization and Visualization

Imagine the person or entity you wish to communicate with in front of you, visualizing them clearly in your mind.

Visualize an energy cord connecting the two of you, representing the telepathic link you are establishing.

Step 5: Sending and Receiving Messages

Mentally focus on the words, thoughts, or images you want to communicate telepathically. Send these messages clearly and intentionally, imagining them flowing along the energy cord.

Be receptive to the responses and information that may come to you. Open yourself to receive telepathic messages intuitively, without judgment or preconceived expectations.

Step 6: Awareness of Signals

Be attentive to any form of telepathic communication you may receive, whether through thoughts, images, emotions, or physical sensations.

Also, observe any insights or intuitions that may arise in your consciousness. Record all relevant experiences and observations in a journal.

Remember, telepathic communication is a subtle skill that may require practice and patience to fully develop. Each individual may have different experiences and results. Maintain an attitude of openness, trust, and curiosity as you explore these techniques. With regular practice and a connection to your intuition, you can enhance your ability to communicate telepathically and establish profound connections beyond physical limitations.

# 47
# Connection with the Inner Self

Step 1: Preparation
Find a quiet and comfortable place where you can concentrate without interruptions. Sit in a relaxed position with your spine straight and your eyes closed.

Begin to relax your body and mind through slow, deep breaths. Allow yourself to release any tension or worry.

Step 2: Inner Tuning
Bring your attention to the present moment and inward. Focus on your breathing, observing the air entering and leaving your body.

Visualize a bright light at the center of your being, representing the essence of your inner self. Feel this light expanding and filling your entire being.

Step 3: Calming the Mind
As you focus on your breathing and inner light, let go of everyday thoughts and worries. Calm your mind, allowing it to become tranquil and serene.

Step 4: Inner Dialogue
Mentally or softly address your inner self, establishing a conscious connection. Use a name or any term that resonates with you to refer to this part of yourself.

Ask your inner self questions, share concerns, or seek guidance and clarity. Be open and receptive to the responses that may arise.

Step 5: Listening and Intuition

Quiet your conscious mind and be receptive to the answers from your inner self. These may manifest as thoughts, insights, images, sensations, or feelings.

Trust your intuition and the innate wisdom of your inner self. Be willing to receive messages and guidance aligned with your well-being and personal growth.

Step 6: Gratitude and Closure

At the end of your communication with your inner self, express gratitude for this valuable connection. Thank your inner self for the guidance and wisdom shared.

Slowly bring your attention back to your surroundings. Gently open your eyes and take a moment to reflect on the experience.

Regular practice of connecting with your inner self can help you develop a deeper relationship with yourself, gain clarity in moments of doubt, and access your inner wisdom. Remember, the connection with your inner self is an individual and unique process for each person. Be open and patient as you explore this practice, allowing the connection to deepen over time with regular practice.

# 48
# Connection with

Step 1: Preparation
Find a quiet Take

Step 2: Intention and Openness
Set the intention to connect with your higher self, also known as your most elevated and wise consciousness.

Open yourself to receive guidance, clarity, and insights from a higher source of wisdom.

Step 3: Energetic Tuning
Visualize a bright light at the center of your being, representing your higher self. Feel this light expanding and filling your entire being.

Allow yourself to connect with this elevated energy and sense its loving and compassionate presence.

Step 4: Dialogue with the Higher Self
Mentally or softly address your higher self, establishing a conscious connection. Use a name or term that resonates with you to refer to this wise part of yourself.

Ask questions, share concerns, or seek guidance and clarity from your higher self. Be open and receptive to the answers that may arise.

Step 5: Inner Listening

Quiet your conscious mind and be receptive to the responses from your higher self. These may manifest as thoughts, insights, images, sensations, or feelings.

Trust the wisdom and guidance of your higher self. Be willing to receive messages that align with your well-being and spiritual growth.

Step 6: Gratitude and Closing

When you conclude your communication with the higher self, express gratitude for this valuable connection. Thank your higher self for the guidance and wisdom shared.

Gradually bring your attention back to your surroundings. Open your eyes gently and take a moment to reflect on the experience.

Connecting with the higher self is a personal and individual practice. Each person may have a unique experience when engaging with this elevated part of themselves. Be patient, trusting, and open as you explore this technique. With regular practice, you can deepen your connection with the higher self and access a source of internal wisdom and guidance.

# 49
# Stillness

Step 1: Preparation
Choose a quiet, distraction-free place where you can sit comfortably. Turn off electronic devices that might interrupt your practice.

Sit in a comfortable position with your spine straight but relaxed. Close your eyes gently or keep a soft gaze fixed on a single point ahead.

Step 2: Breath Awareness
Direct your attention to your breathing. Notice the flow of air entering and exiting your body. Feel the expansion and contraction of your abdomen or the air passing through your nostrils.

Do not try to control your breathing; simply observe it naturally, letting it be the focus of your attention.

Step 3: Observing Thoughts
As you focus on your breath, notice the thoughts that arise in your mind. Avoid engaging with or judging these thoughts. Just observe them passing by, like clouds in the sky.

If you find yourself getting caught up in a thought, gently return your attention to your breath and let the thought dissolve.

Step 4: Cultivating Inner Stillness

As you continue observing your breath and thoughts, you may begin to notice moments of silence and inner stillness. Allow yourself to rest in these moments of tranquility without clinging to or prolonging them.

Let the stillness permeate your being, allowing a sense of calm and serenity to grow within you.

Step 5: Acceptance and Non-Judgment

Practice acceptance and non-judgment toward the thoughts, emotions, or sensations that arise during the practice. Let everything be as it is, without resistance or struggle.

Remember, stillness is not the complete absence of thought but rather a connection to a state of inner peace even amidst mental activity.

Step 6: Time to Close

At the end of the practice, take a moment to thank yourself for dedicating time to cultivating stillness. Gradually bring your attention back to your surroundings.

Open your eyes gently and allow yourself to integrate the effects of the practice into your day.

Regular stillness practice can help calm the mind, reduce stress, and cultivate a state of presence and serenity. Remember that stillness is a continuous process, and each session may differ. Over time, you may develop a greater capacity to connect with inner peace and bring that sense of calm into all areas of your life.

# 50
# Self-Connection

Step 1: Preparation
Find a quiet place where you can focus without interruptions. Sit or lie down in a comfortable position, keeping your spine straight.

Close your eyes and begin relaxing your body and mind through slow, deep breaths. Let go of thoughts and worries, focusing on the present moment.

Step 2: Body Awareness
Turn your attention to your body. Mentally scan all parts of your body from head to toe, observing physical sensations.

Be present with the sensations, without judgment or desire for change. Simply observe and allow yourself to connect with your body.

Step 3: Emotional Exploration
Shift your attention to the emotions present within you. Identify any emotions that may arise at the moment and observe them without judgment.

Allow yourself to fully feel these emotions, acknowledging them as part of your human experience. Take deep breaths and let the emotions flow.

Step 4: Inner Dialogue

Initiate an internal dialogue with yourself. Ask questions like: "How am I feeling? What do I need right now? What is my inner truth?"

Listen carefully to the answers that emerge. Be open to insights and intuitions that may arise from within.

Step 5: Practice of Self-Compassion

Cultivate self-compassion by nurturing yourself with love and kindness. Acknowledge your struggles, challenges, and imperfections, and treat yourself with gentleness and understanding.

Send positive thoughts and affirmations to yourself. Allow yourself to embrace all parts of who you are, accepting your humanity.

Step 6: Gratitude and Closing

As you conclude the practice of self-connection, take a moment to express gratitude for yourself and the opportunity to connect with your inner being.

Gradually bring your attention back to your surroundings. Open your eyes gently and reflect on the experience.

Regular self-connection practice can strengthen your relationship with yourself, nurture authenticity and self-compassion, and foster greater self-awareness. Remember that self-connection is a unique and individual process. Be open and patient as you explore these techniques, allowing your connection with yourself to deepen over time and with regular practice.

# 51
# Energy Healing

Step 1: Preparation
Find a quiet place where you can focus without interruptions. Sit or lie down in a comfortable position, keeping your spine straight.

Close your eyes and begin relaxing your body and mind through slow, deep breaths. Let go of thoughts and worries, focusing on the present moment.

Step 2: Energy Awareness
Turn your attention to your inner energy. Feel the aura surrounding your body and notice the sensation of energy flowing within you.

Observe any sensations, vibrations, or energy blockages that may be present. Be curious and open to the energetic experience.

Step 3: Intention and Focus
Set a clear intention for energy healing. This can be directed to a specific area of the body, emotions, or overall well-being.

Focus your attention on this healing intention, allowing it to manifest in your awareness and expand throughout your being.

Step 4: Energy Direction

Using your hands, begin directing energy to the area you wish to heal. Feel the energy flowing from your hands, channeling it to the specific location.

Use slow and gentle movements, maintaining a clear intention of healing as you direct the energy. Visualize the energy enveloping and filling the area.

Step 5: Cleansing and Balancing

As you direct the energy, visualize it clearing away blockages, removing stagnant or negative energy, and bringing balance to the area.

Feel the energy restoring harmony and healthy flow, promoting healing and well-being at all levels.

Step 6: Gratitude and Closing

When you finish the energy healing practice, take a moment to express gratitude for the opportunity to connect with healing energy and for the healing process that has taken place.

Gradually bring your attention back to your surroundings. Open your eyes gently and take a moment to reflect on the experience.

Regular energy healing practice can help balance, harmonize, and strengthen the body's vital energy. Remember that energy healing is a personal and unique process for each individual. Be open and confident in your ability to work with energy to promote healing. Over time, practice, and intention, you can develop a deeper connection with healing energy and use this technique to support your well-being.

# 52
# Cosmic Healing

Step 1: Preparation
Find a quiet place where you can focus without interruptions. Sit or lie down in a comfortable position, keeping your spine straight.

Close your eyes and begin to relax your body and mind with deep, slow breaths. Let go of thoughts and worries, focusing on the present moment.

Step 2: Connection with the Cosmos
Visualize yourself surrounded by a sphere of cosmic light. Feel this light flowing through and around you, connecting you with the vastness of the universe.

Sense yourself as an integral part of the cosmos, connected to all universal energies and forces.

Step 3: Intention and Focus
Set a clear intention for the cosmic healing. It can be directed at yourself, other people, or the planet as a whole.

Focus your attention on this healing intention, allowing it to manifest in your consciousness and expand to embrace the cosmic dimension.

Step 4: Channeling Cosmic Energy
Visualize cosmic energy flowing into and through you. Feel it as a bright, loving light that brings healing, harmony, and balance.

Allow this cosmic energy to flow where it is needed, whether in your body, others, or the Earth as a whole.

Step 5: Transmitting the Healing

As you connect with the cosmic energy, direct it to the area or situation you wish to heal. Visualize the cosmic energy surrounding and filling this space, bringing healing and transformation.

See yourself as a channel, allowing the energy to flow through you and be transmitted with love and the intention of healing.

Step 6: Gratitude and Closing

When concluding the cosmic healing practice, take a moment to express gratitude for the opportunity to connect with the cosmic healing energy and for the transformation that has occurred.

Slowly bring your awareness back to your surroundings. Gently open your eyes and take a moment to reflect on the experience.

Regular practice of cosmic healing can help expand your consciousness, connect with universal energies, and bring healing and transformation to yourself, others, and the planet. Remember, cosmic healing is a co-creative process with universal energies, and each experience may be unique. Be open, receptive, and confident in your ability to work with cosmic energy to promote healing and well-being.

# 53
# Astral Travel and Interdimensional Encounters

Step 1: Preparation

Find a quiet, safe place where you can practice without being disturbed. Choose a time of day when you are relaxed yet alert.

Create an atmosphere conducive to practice, using soft music, aromatherapy, or any other element that helps relax and induce an altered state of consciousness.

Step 2: Deep Relaxation

Sit or lie in a comfortable position. Begin to consciously relax your body, starting from your feet and slowly moving up to your head.

Release muscle tension, breathe deeply, and exhale slowly. Allow yourself to enter a deep state of physical and mental relaxation.

Step 3: Intention Focus

Set a clear intention for your astral travel or interdimensional encounter. Visualize the place or dimension you wish to explore or the being you wish to connect with.

Hold this intention in your mind and heart, letting it strengthen as you prepare for the experience.

Step 4: Induction Techniques

Explore various techniques for inducing astral travel, such as the heavy body technique, the climbing technique, the separation technique, and others.

Try different methods to find what works best for you. Some involve active imagination, visualization, or repetition of affirmations.

Step 5: Experience Control

During astral travel or interdimensional encounters, it is important to remain calm and in control. Remember that you are in an altered state of consciousness, which may be challenging at first.

Stay focused on your intention and avoid distractions from other thoughts or stimuli. Be open and receptive to the experiences that arise but maintain a level of discernment.

Step 6: Return and Integration

At the end of the experience, remember to express gratitude for the insights or experiences you've received. Thank the universe, guides, or beings you interacted with.

Gradually bring your awareness back to your physical body. Allow yourself to integrate the experiences and insights gained during the astral travel or interdimensional encounter.

Practicing these techniques requires time and dedication. Experiences may not always be immediate or linear. Be patient with yourself and open to possibilities. If needed, seek guidance from experienced individuals or communities with similar interests.

# 54
# Consciousness Expansion

Step 1: Preparation
Find a quiet place where you can focus without interruptions. Sit or lie down in a comfortable position, keeping your spine straight.

Close your eyes and start to relax your body and mind with deep, slow breaths. Let go of thoughts and worries, focusing on the present moment.

Step 2: Deep Relaxation
Fully relax your body, starting from your feet and slowly moving to your head. Release muscle tension and breathe deeply.

As you deepen your relaxation, allow your mind to calm down and enter a state of receptivity.

Step 3: Expanding Perception
Focus on the present moment and your physical body. Become aware of your physical sensations, such as breathing, heartbeat, and any other sensations.

Then, expand your awareness beyond your physical body, becoming conscious of your surroundings. Notice the sounds, smells, and sensations in the environment, allowing yourself to feel a broader connection with everything around you.

Step 4: Inner Exploration

Turn your attention inward. Observe your thoughts, emotions, and internal sensations. Be open and receptive to any experience that arises, without judgment or resistance.

Explore different layers of your consciousness, delving deeper into your inner self. Be willing to connect with parts of yourself that may be forgotten or hidden.

Step 5: Connection with Universal Consciousness

Open yourself to an expanded consciousness that transcends individual limits. Feel connected to the universal consciousness and the interconnected fabric of all things.

Allow yourself to feel this connection and unity with the universe, recognizing yourself as a unique and valuable expression of this greater consciousness.

Step 6: Integration and Gratitude

At the end of the consciousness expansion practice, take a moment to reflect on the experience. Recognize any insights, understanding, or transformation that occurred.

Feel gratitude for the opportunity to expand your consciousness and deepen your connection with yourself and the universe. Express gratitude for the ongoing process of growth and learning.

Regular practice of consciousness expansion techniques can lead to greater awareness of yourself, others, and the universe as a whole. Be open, patient, and receptive to the experiences that arise during this journey. Remember that each person may have a unique and valuable experience, and there is no right or wrong way to expand consciousness.

# 55
# DNA Activation

Step 1: Preparation
Find a quiet place where you can focus without interruptions. Sit or lie down in a comfortable position, keeping your spine straight.

Take a few deep breaths to relax your body and mind, letting go of thoughts and worries.

Step 2: Intention
Set a clear intention for DNA activation. You may wish to awaken and access your full human potential, enhance your spiritual awareness, or promote healing and balance on all levels.

Keep this intention in your heart and mind throughout the process.

Step 3: Visualization
Close your eyes and begin to visualize a stream of pure white light descending from the cosmos and moving through the top of your head (crown chakra).

See this light gently entering your body, flowing through every cell, organ, and system of your being.

Step 4: Mantras and Affirmations
As you visualize the light flowing through your body, repeat mantras or affirmations that resonate with you. For example, say, "I activate my DNA for the

highest potential of love, wisdom, and healing," or any other affirmation aligned with your intention.

Feel the vibration and energy of the words as you repeat them, allowing them to integrate into your being.

Step 5: Conscious Breathing

Focus on your breathing and begin to breathe consciously. Inhale deeply through your nose and exhale through your mouth, letting the life force energy flow through you.

As you breathe, imagine each inhalation activating and energizing your DNA, expanding your awareness and connecting you with your higher self.

Step 6: Gratitude and Closing

At the end of the DNA activation practice, take a moment to express gratitude for the experience and the opportunity to expand and awaken your potential.

Visualize the bright light filling your entire being and radiating out to the world around you, sharing love and positive energy.

Remember, DNA activation is a continuous and gradual process. Regular practice and openness to receive changes and insights are essential. Be willing to connect with your higher self, trusting in your individual process of evolution and growth.

Note: The concept of DNA activation is often associated with spiritual and metaphysical perspectives. Approach these practices with an open mind and personal discernment.

# 56
# Conscious Breathing

Step 1: Preparation
Find a quiet and comfortable place where you can sit or lie down undisturbed. Ensure your spine is straight, allowing the air to flow freely.
Close your eyes or keep them slightly open, softly gazing at a fixed point ahead of you.

Step 2: Breath Awareness
Begin by directing your attention to your breathing. Observe the natural flow of air as it enters and exits your body.
Focus on the sensation of the breath at your nostrils, the movement of your abdomen, or the flow of air through your airways.

Step 3: Deep Breathing
Start breathing more deeply, inhaling slowly through your nose and exhaling through your mouth. Feel the air filling your lungs and allow yourself to relax further with each exhalation.
As you breathe deeply, try to expand your abdomen during the inhalation and gently contract it during the exhalation.

Step 4: Rhythm and Counting
To help focus your mind and establish a rhythm, you can count your breaths. For example, inhale

counting to four, hold the breath for a moment, and then exhale counting to four again.

Maintain a comfortable and natural rhythm, adjusting the count as needed.

Step 5: Observation Without Judgment

As you practice conscious breathing, be aware of any thoughts, emotions, or physical sensations that arise. Observe them without judgment, allowing them to come and go like clouds passing in the sky.

If your mind wanders, gently bring your attention back to your breathing without worrying about interruptions or distractions.

Step 6: Relaxation and Presence

As you continue conscious breathing, allow yourself to relax even more with each exhalation. Feel your mind calming and your awareness expanding in the present moment.

Be fully present in your experience of breathing, letting go of past or future concerns. Just be, breathing consciously.

Regular practice of conscious breathing can help calm the mind, reduce stress, and promote a greater sense of awareness in the present moment. You can practice this technique for a few minutes daily or whenever you need a moment of tranquility and connection with yourself.

Remember, each person's experience with conscious breathing is unique, so adapt the technique to what works best for you.

# 57
# Cellular Regeneration

Step 1: Preparation
Find a quiet place where you can sit or lie down comfortably, undisturbed. Ensure your spine is straight to facilitate breathing and energy flow.

Close your eyes or keep them slightly open, softly gazing at a fixed point ahead of you.

Step 2: Relaxation
Begin relaxing your body and mind through slow, deep breaths. Allow any tension or stress to be released with each exhalation.

Focus on relaxing each part of your body, from your feet to your head. Feel yourself sinking into a deep sense of calm and tranquility.

Step 3: Intention and Focus
Set a clear intention for cellular regeneration, focusing on healing and rejuvenating your body at the cellular level.

Visualize your body's cells renewing and regenerating with vitality and health. See them glowing with a bright, radiant light.

Step 4: Energetic Breathing
Begin breathing deeply and consciously, paying attention to your breath. As you inhale, imagine you are bringing vital, healing energy into your body.

Visualize this energy flowing into each cell, nourishing and revitalizing them. Feel yourself filled with this healing energy with every inhalation.

Step 5: Visualization and Affirmations

As you breathe, visualize each cell in your body renewing and regenerating. See them becoming vibrant and healthy, restoring to their optimal state.

Accompany this visualization with positive affirmations such as "My cells regenerate with health and vitality," "My body is a vessel of healing and rejuvenation," or other phrases that resonate with you.

Step 6: Gratitude and Closure

As you complete the practice of cellular regeneration, take a moment to express gratitude for your body and the healing process taking place.

Thank your cells for their vital functions and regenerative capabilities. Feel full of gratitude and love for yourself and your body.

Regular practice of cellular regeneration can help promote health, well-being, and vitality in your body. Remember that visualization and affirmations are powerful ways to direct energy and intention, and consistent practice can bring positive results over time.

# 58
# Connecting with the Star Child Within

Step 1: Self-Questioning and Reflection
Take a quiet moment to self-reflect and ask yourself if you feel deeply connected to the cosmos, if you sense a belonging to something greater than just Earth, and if you feel different or special in some way.

Observe your life experiences, perceptions, and intuitions. Pay attention to any unique characteristics, abilities, or gifts you may have.

Step 2: Research and Exploration
Research and study the traits associated with "Star Children." This may include information about star origins, soul missions, intuitive abilities, environmental sensitivity, deep empathy, spiritual connections, and more.

As you learn about these traits, see if they resonate with you and align with your own experiences and inner sensations.

Step 3: Self-Connection and Intuition
Practice quiet moments of introspection to connect with your inner self. This can be done through meditation, silent contemplation, or other practices that help calm the mind and open the heart.

Notice what insights, intuitions, or feelings arise during these moments of self-connection. Pay special attention to any information indicating a connection to the stars or a cosmic origin.

Step 4: Seeking Community

Look for online communities or local groups dedicated to studying and discussing "Star Children." Connect with others who may have similar experiences and share knowledge and stories.

Participate in discussions, ask questions, and share your own experiences to deepen your understanding and feel supported in this journey of discovery.

Step 5: Integration and Acceptance

Remember that identifying as a "Star Child" is a personal and unique journey for each individual. Regardless of the outcome, be open to accepting and integrating your own experiences and perceptions.

Recognize that we are all cosmic beings connected to the universe in diverse and meaningful ways, whether or not we explicitly identify as "Star Children."

Approach this exploration with an open mind and a healthy dose of discernment. Remember that self-discovery is an ongoing process and that you are the best authority on your own spiritual journey.

# 59
# Accessing the Stellar Portal

Step 1: Preparation and Intention

Find a quiet place where you can sit or lie down comfortably, undisturbed. Ensure your spine is straight to facilitate breathing and energy flow.

Set a clear intention to connect with a Stellar Portal. Visualize yourself open and receptive to the energy and experiences that may arise during the process.

Step 2: Meditation and Relaxation

Begin a meditation practice to relax your mind and calm your body. This can be done through conscious breathing techniques, guided visualizations, or any method you are comfortable with.

Allow your mind to quiet and open to a sense of tranquility and receptivity. Let go of daily thoughts and worries.

Step 3: Visualization and Intention

Visualize a Stellar Portal before you, perhaps a portal of light, a dimensional gateway, or any image that resonates with you. Feel the pulsating and powerful energy emanating from the portal.

Deepen your intention to connect with stellar beings and energies. Feel your heart open and allow yourself to be enveloped by this stellar energy.

Step 4: Permission and Surrender

Declare aloud or internally your intention to allow stellar energies to connect with you. Open yourself to receiving messages, insights, or experiences that may arise during the process.

Be open and receptive, trusting in the flow of energies and your own discernment.

Step 5: Exploration and Communication

As you connect with the Stellar Portal, feel free to explore and interact with the energies and stellar beings present. Ask questions, share your intention, and open yourself to receiving guidance or insights.

Pay attention to any information, images, feelings, or knowledge that may emerge during this time of connection. Trust your intuition and allow yourself to experience authentically.

Step 6: Closure and Gratitude

When you feel ready to conclude the practice, thank the stellar beings, the Stellar Portal, and yourself for the experience.

Return your awareness to your physical body, move gently, and take a moment to integrate any learnings or insights you received.

Remember that accessing the Stellar Portal is a personal and unique experience for each individual. Regular practice and openness to these experiences can lead to greater contact with stellar energies and beings. Trust your own journey and follow your intuition as you explore this path of cosmic connection.

# 60
# Energy Transmutation

Step 1: Energy Awareness

Become aware of the energies around you, both internally and externally. Observe your own emotions, thoughts, and physical sensations. Also notice the energies present in your environment and in your interactions with others.

Recognize that all energies have a unique vibration and quality.

Step 2: Intention and Focus

Set a clear intention to transmute and transform negative energies into positive ones. Establish the intention to work with energies in a beneficial way for yourself and others.

Focus your attention on specific areas where you sense negative or blocked energies that need transmutation.

Step 3: Visualization and Alchemy

Visualize yourself surrounded by white, golden, or colorful light, representing pure and transformative energy. Feel this light permeating your entire being, filling you with a sense of peace, love, and harmony.

Imagine this light expanding beyond you, enveloping the negative energies you identified. See these energies dissolving and transforming into pure positive light.

Step 4: Conscious Breathing

Use your breath as a tool for energy transmutation. Inhale deeply, visualizing pure light entering your body. As you exhale, release any negative energy, allowing it to be transmuted by the light.

Continue this process of conscious breathing, letting the pure light fill every cell of your body and transmute any negative energy present.

Step 5: Intention of Love and Healing

Set an intention of love and healing for all the energies involved in the transmutation process. Feel deep compassion for these energies, acknowledging that they are also part of the whole.

Wrap the transmuted energies in an intention of healing and harmony, wishing them to find balance and integrate into the universal flow of love and light.

Step 6: Regular Practice and Self-Care

Energy transmutation is a continuous practice. Set aside time regularly to perform these techniques, as they will help keep your energy field clean and balanced.

Additionally, take care of yourself by practicing self-care and developing a healthy routine. This includes adequate rest, nutritious food, relaxation practices, and activities that promote overall well-being.

Remember, energy transmutation is an individual process, and everyone can find their own approaches and techniques. Trust your intuition and adjust the practices according to what resonates with you. As you become more skilled in energy transmutation, you can create a more harmonious and vibrant internal and external environment.

# 61
# Grounding

Step 1: Body Awareness

Begin by becoming aware of your physical body. Sit or stand comfortably. Close your eyes and take a few deep breaths to relax.

Feel the contact of your body with the chair, the floor, or any surface you are resting on. Notice physical sensations like pressure, weight, and warmth.

Step 2: Connection to the Earth

Visualize roots growing from your feet (or from the base of your spine if you're seated). These roots extend deep into the ground, connecting with the Earth's core.

Feel the Earth's energy rising through the roots, flowing into your body. This energy is stable, strong, and grounding.

Step 3: Breathing and Intention

Use your breath to strengthen your grounding. As you inhale, imagine pulling Earth energy upward into your body. As you exhale, let this energy spread throughout your body, filling it with vitality.

Set a clear intention to ground yourself in the present moment and to be fully present in your body. Focus on being completely here and now, releasing worries or scattered thoughts.

Step 4: Grounding Visualization

Visualize a strong and stable anchor descending from your base (feet or spine) toward the Earth's center. This anchor is made of durable material, like metal or crystal.

See this anchor securing itself deeply into the Earth's core, providing a safe and stable connection.

Step 5: Integration and Expansion

Feel the sensation of being rooted and grounded. Notice how this connection to the Earth brings stability, security, and balance to your body and mind.

From this grounded state, allow yourself to expand and interact with the world around you. Feel rooted while remaining open to receiving and sharing energy.

Step 6: Regular Practice

Grounding is a practice that can be incorporated into your daily routine. Take a few minutes each day to connect with the Earth and reinforce your grounding.

Additionally, during moments of stress, anxiety, or imbalance, consciously ground yourself to help restore emotional and mental stability.

Remember, grounding is a powerful tool for balancing your energies and connecting with the present. Practice regularly and adapt the techniques to your personal preferences. When grounded, you'll face life's challenges with greater stability and clarity.

# 62
# Arcturian Resonance

Step 1: Intention and Openness

Set a clear intention to attune and resonate with Arcturian energies. Be open and receptive to receiving the messages and vibrational frequencies of the Arcturians.

Be willing to connect with the love, wisdom, and healing they offer.

Step 2: Preparation and Environment

Choose a quiet place where you can sit or lie comfortably. Ensure the space is clean and free of distractions. You may light candles, burn incense, or use crystals to create a sacred atmosphere if you wish.

Turn off or minimize any external noise sources, such as phones or televisions.

Step 3: Meditation and Relaxation

Begin a meditation practice to calm your mind and relax your body. This can be done through conscious breathing, guided visualizations, or any method you feel comfortable with.

Allow your mind to quiet and enter a receptive meditative state. Open yourself to the experience of tuning into Arcturian energies.

Step 4: Attunement to Arcturian Frequency

Visualize a bright, bluish light enveloping your entire being. Feel this light permeating every cell of your body, bringing peace, harmony, and unconditional love.

Open your heart to receive Arcturian vibrational frequencies. Imagine yourself attuning to the Arcturian collective consciousness, allowing their wisdom and healing to flow into you.

Step 5: Communication and Interaction

Ask questions or share your intentions with the Arcturians, whether through thoughts, spoken words, or writing.

Be open to receiving messages, insights, guidance, or physical sensations that may arise during your practice. Trust your intuition and immerse yourself in the experience of Arcturian resonance.

Step 6: Closure and Gratitude

When you feel it's time to conclude, thank the Arcturians and the energies you've connected with. Express gratitude for the wisdom and healing you received.

Return to your present awareness, move gently, and take a moment to reflect on your experience. Note any insights or information you've gained.

Remember, Arcturian resonance is a personal and unique experience for each individual. Practice regularly and trust your own intuition and discernment. As you deepen this practice, you may develop a more meaningful connection with the Arcturians and their energies of love and healing.

# 63
# Self-Knowledge

Step 1: Intention and Openness

Set a clear intention to seek self-knowledge and be open to exploring yourself honestly and compassionately. Be willing to understand yourself on a deeper level, including your thoughts, emotions, beliefs, and behavior patterns.

Be open to receiving insights and better understanding who you are.

Step 2: Reflection and Self-Inquiry

Take time for reflection and self-inquiry. Ask yourself deep questions about your life experiences, motivations, values, and aspirations. Challenge limiting beliefs and repetitive patterns.

Write your reflections in a journal or notebook, as this helps clarify your thoughts and document your discoveries.

Step 3: Practices of Self-Connection

Dedicate time to practices that help you connect with yourself, such as meditation, yoga, nature walks, art, or any activity that allows you to be present and in tune with your essence.

Explore different techniques and find those that resonate with you, providing moments of silence, introspection, and self-reflection.

Step 4: Conscious Self-Observation

Cultivate the ability to observe yourself with awareness and without judgment. Notice your thoughts, emotions, and behaviors without becoming fully engaged with them. Become a neutral observer of yourself.

Pay attention to your patterns and automatic reactions. By observing yourself objectively, you can identify areas for growth and change.

Step 5: Acceptance and Compassion

Practice acceptance and compassion for yourself. Recognize that you are a constantly evolving human being, and we all have strengths and weaknesses. Be kind to yourself as you uncover parts of yourself that may be challenging or difficult.

Embrace all aspects of your being with love and understanding.

Step 6: Seeking External Knowledge

Seek external knowledge through books, courses, lectures, therapy, or any other source that can provide insights and perspectives on self-knowledge.

Be open to learning from different philosophies, spiritual practices, therapeutic approaches, or belief systems that resonate with you and aid in your self-discovery journey.

Step 7: Integration and Self-Transformation

As you gain knowledge about yourself, look for ways to integrate these discoveries into your daily life.

Identify areas where you want to grow and develop, and take concrete steps toward positive change.

Be open to transformation as you come to know yourself better, leveraging self-knowledge to live a more authentic and meaningful life.

Remember, the journey of self-knowledge is continuous and non-linear. Practice regularly and be patient with yourself. As you deepen your self-knowledge, you will cultivate a deeper connection with yourself and the world around you.

# 64
# Recognizing Gifts

Step 1: Self-Exploration and Self-Awareness

Take time for self-exploration and developing self-awareness. Observe your interests, skills, and areas of curiosity. Pay attention to activities in which you naturally excel and that bring you joy and satisfaction.

Make a list of things you enjoy doing and feel comfortable with. Write down any talents or skills you have already identified in yourself.

Step 2: Experimentation and Exploration

Give yourself permission to experiment and explore different areas of interest. Try new activities, attend workshops, take courses, or find mentors who can guide you in your discovery process.

Be open to stepping out of your comfort zone and trying new things. Sometimes, you may discover a hidden gift by exploring areas you've never considered before.

Step 3: Observing Reactions and Feedback

Observe how people around you react when you are engaged in specific activities. Pay attention to compliments, positive comments, and feedback you receive. These can provide valuable clues about your natural gifts. Be open to constructive feedback and others' perspectives. Sometimes, others may see talents and abilities in you that you haven't noticed yourself.

Step 4: Following Passion and Flow

Pay attention to activities that energize you and make you lose track of time. These are the activities where you may be expressing your natural gifts.

Notice how you feel when immersed in an activity. The sense of flow, enthusiasm, and joy can indicate that you are connected with your gifts.

Step 5: Self-Reflection and Self-Evaluation

Take time to reflect on your strengths and talents. Make a list of things you do well and the skills others recognize in you. Evaluate how these gifts can be applied in different areas of your life, such as work, relationships, hobbies, or community service.

Step 6: Cultivate and Enhance Your Gifts

Once you've identified your gifts, find ways to cultivate and enhance them. This can be done through regular practice, education, training, or mentorship.

Look for opportunities to share your gifts with others and find ways to apply them in your daily life.

Remember, recognizing your gifts is an individual process and may take time. Be patient with yourself and trust your intuition. As you tune into your natural gifts, you may find a greater sense of purpose and fulfillment in life.

# 65
# Radiating Arcturian Light

Step 1: Preparation and Intention
Find a quiet space where you can sit or lie down comfortably. Ensure you will not be interrupted during the practice.

Set a clear intention to radiate Arcturian light for your benefit and the well-being of all beings involved. Visualize yourself as a channel of light, connected to Arcturian energies and ready to radiate them.

Step 2: Attunement and Connection
Close your eyes and begin deep breathing, allowing your body to relax. Connect with your breath and enter a state of calm and tranquility.

Visualize a bright white light descending from above and enveloping your entire being. Feel this pure and loving light penetrating every cell in your body, purifying and strengthening your energy.

Step 3: Activation of Arcturian Light
Visualize a vibrant blue beam of light descending from the sky, entering the top of your head, and flowing through your body. Feel this light expanding and filling your entire being.

As the Arcturian light fills you, allow yourself to absorb its qualities of healing, wisdom, and unconditional love. Feel connected to Arcturian consciousness and let it flow through you.

Step 4: Radiating Arcturian Light

Visualize yourself surrounded by a field of radiant Arcturian light. As you breathe, imagine this light expanding beyond your body, radiating into your surroundings.

Allow the Arcturian light to extend beyond physical space, encompassing your community, country, and the entire world. Visualize the Arcturian light bringing healing, peace, and harmony to all beings.

Step 5: Intention for Healing and Transformation

While radiating Arcturian light, direct your intention toward healing and transformation. Send love and healing to all beings who are suffering, to areas of conflict, and for the healing of the planet as a whole.

Visualize the Arcturian light dissolving any negative energies, traumas, or blockages, replacing them with light and love. See the healing spreading and touching the lives of all beings.

Step 6: Gratitude and Closure

As you conclude the practice, express gratitude to the Arcturian energies for their presence and assistance in radiating the light. Thank them for allowing you to be a channel of light and contribute to the world's healing and transformation.

Return to your present awareness, open your eyes, and carry the sense of connection with the Arcturian light throughout your day.

Remember, radiating Arcturian light is a practice aimed at bringing healing, love, and transformation. Practice regularly and allow yourself to explore this connection with Arcturian energies on your spiritual growth journey.

# 66
# The Ascension of Consciousness

Step 1: Cultivate Present Moment Awareness

Practice mindfulness and full attention in your daily activities. Be fully present in the moment, aware of your sensations, thoughts, and emotions.

Develop the ability to observe your thought patterns and automatic reactions without fully engaging with them. Become a neutral observer of your own mind and emotions.

Step 2: Expand Your Consciousness

Explore different spiritual practices that can help expand your consciousness, such as meditation, yoga, visualizations, and conscious breathing techniques. These practices can help open your mind to subtler levels of perception and awareness.

Step 3: Self-Questioning and Self-Reflection

Ask profound questions about the purpose of your life, your beliefs, values, and identity. Question the assumptions and limiting patterns that may be restricting your consciousness.

Take time regularly for self-reflection and analysis of your experiences, learning from them, and seeking to grow and evolve as a human being.

Step 4: Pursue Knowledge

Seek knowledge in various areas, such as philosophy, spirituality, psychology, and science. Explore different spiritual traditions and philosophical perspectives to expand your understanding of the world and yourself.

Be open to learning from others and willing to challenge your own beliefs and established concepts.

Step 5: Practice Love and Compassion

Cultivate love and compassion for yourself and all beings. Practice acts of kindness and generosity. Develop the ability to see humanity as one interconnected family.

Be aware of how your actions affect others and always strive to act with compassion and empathy.

Step 6: Tune into Inner Wisdom

Connect with your intuition and inner wisdom. Learn to trust your inner voice and follow its guidance. Allow your intuition to guide your choices and decisions.

Step 7: Integration and Self-Transformation

As your consciousness expands, seek to incorporate the insights and knowledge gained into your daily life. Strive for self-transformation, working to align your actions and behaviors with your expanded vision of yourself and the world.

Remember, the ascension of consciousness is a continuous and individual process. Respect your own pace and be open to growing and evolving over time.

Allow yourself to dive into this journey of expanding consciousness with curiosity, humility, and love.

# Acknowledgments

Dear reader,

I would like to express my deep gratitude for following this guide of techniques. Energy healing is a personal and meaningful journey that requires dedication, openness, and perseverance, and I am happy to have shared this information with you.

Remember that the paths are unique for each individual, and you have the power to explore and discover your own inner truth. By practicing the techniques presented, you are taking an important step toward awakening your highest potential.

The pursuit of self-knowledge, healing, and spiritual evolution is a continuous journey, and I hope these techniques have provided you with a valuable starting point. I encourage you to continue exploring, learning, and growing at your own pace.

I sincerely thank you for your dedication to seeking a deeper understanding of yourself and the world around you. May you find peace, joy, and inspiration on your journey of ascending consciousness.

www.ingramcontent.com/pod-product-compliance
Lightning Source LLC
LaVergne TN
LVHW041940070526
838199LV00051BA/2857